THE WORLD'S EASIEST RECIPES

Five Ingredients

Linda Duncan

T0382012

HarperCollinsPublishers

harpercollins.co.nz

BREAKFAST & LUNCH

MAINS

SALADS & SIDES

DESSERTS

INTRODUCTION

Welcome to my cookbook, *The World's Easiest Recipes*. I am deeply honoured that you have chosen to explore the pages of my culinary journey, and I sincerely hope you discover a wealth of fresh inspiration within these pages.

I started my cookbook writing journey just over six years ago while I was still working with my husband Wayne in our accounting business in Taupo, New Zealand. It was a time of reflection for me as we had recently become empty nesters, and I started to wonder how I managed to get through the many years of being a busy parents of three while running a business. I felt an overwhelming desire to write a cookbook that helped other busy parents cope with the never-ending task of feeding their families on both a financial and time restrained budget. Slowly my brand, 'The World's Easiest Recipes' came to life and now six years down the track I am onto my fifth endeavour.

I would firstly like to point out that I don't consider myself a foodie but someone who loves simple home cooking. If you come to my place for dinner, you are highly unlikely to be served slow-roasted quail and baked Alaska, but more likely to see spaghetti and meatballs and apple crumble on your plates. I love to cook using humble, inexpensive ingredients that feed the soul and warm the heart. I love my family and guests to feel welcomed, relaxed and leave with full stomachs and a sense of feeling uplifted.

There are two things I look for in a recipe. One is a short list of everyday ingredients. If I see a recipe with a long list of ingredients my eyes glaze over. The other thing I look for is easy-to-follow and to-the-point instructions. If a recipe has long-winded instructions, I get brain freeze and I automatically assume the recipe is difficult to prepare.

Writing a cookbook using no more than five ingredients in each recipe is something I have always wanted to achieve. I have loved every minute spent writing this book and I am very excited to share the recipes with you. It goes to prove that you don't need lots of fancy ingredients to create a delicious meal. I have cheated a little bit, not counting pantry staples – such as olive oil, salt and pepper, flour for thickening, water and optional garnishes – in this limit. You will notice that the other ingredients are those with big flavours, like parmesan and feta, balsamic vinegar, herbs, spice blends, relish, Marmite, soy sauce, mustard, sweet chilli sauce, Worcestershire sauce, lemons, chocolate and vanilla extract just to name a few. As you can see, they are all everyday, economical ingredients available at any supermarket, many of which I am sure you will already have in your pantry.

People often tell me they can't cook. My answer to them is simple; everyone can cook if they have the right recipes. I think many people have been put off cooking because they have tried many times but have failed. The reason they failed was probably because the recipes were beyond their ability.

The truth is, cooking is a skill that can be cultivated with the right guidance. If you are new to cooking, I am sure this cookbook will act as your supportive guide that will instil confidence in the kitchen and make you realise cooking can be an enjoyable and rewarding experience. On the other hand, if you are a skilled and experienced cook, sometimes you may crave the simplicity of easy recipes that showcase the pure essence of basic ingredients. These recipes will provide a welcome break, allowing seasoned cooks to unwind while preparing something comforting and uncomplicated.

In a world where we can fill our kitchens up with every gadget and appliance under the sun, I like to use only a handful of basic items. A decent garlic crusher, kitchen knife set and hand-held stick blender are items that are worth paying a little more money for and will become your best friends in the kitchen. They are an investment and will last for many years. A sharp chef's knife is indispensable; it's not just a tool, but an extension of the cook's hand, enabling precise chopping, slicing and dicing.

A sturdy cutting board provides a stable surface for various food preparations and protects both your benchtop and knives. A set of stainless-steel pots and pans ensures even cooking and durability, while a non-stick frying pan is perfect for everything from omelettes to stir-fried veggies. A high-quality whisk makes blending, beating and whipping an ease. For baking enthusiasts, baking paper is a versatile kitchen essential used to line baking trays and pans, to prevent sticking and making clean-up a breeze.

My husband and I spend a lot of time in our campervan. With limited space, we keep only one pot, a frying pan and a single bowl on board. Despite these constraints, I find immense satisfaction in cooking uncomplicated meals, embracing minimalism but still enjoying delicious meals while on the road. Testament that with even the most basic kitchen items cooking well is possible.

I recently purchased an air fryer, which I was very sceptical about at first. I thought it was going to be another appliance gathering dust in my pantry, but how wrong I was. While it might not be essential, my husband and I, now living alone, have found it incredibly beneficial. The air fryer has proven to be a time and money saver, sparing me the daily chore of turning on the oven. Its convenience makes it a valuable addition, especially for those living alone or in small households, making cooking simpler and more efficient.

I aspire for this cookbook to not only enhance your everyday cooking but also kindle the inspiration to gather your loved ones around the table. By preparing straightforward yet delicious meals, you can host family and friends without straining your budget or exhausting yourself. There's something truly special about the bonding that occurs over a shared, uncomplicated meal, a genuine effortless connection that brings people together in the warmest way possible.

Linda
x

TEMPERATURES AND MEASUREMENTS

OVEN TEMPERATURES

All oven temperatures are stated using normal bake settings. Reduce the temperature by 20°C if using a fan bake setting. All temperatures are a guide only, as each oven varies.

PANTRY STAPLES

The recipes in this book use five or fewer key ingredients but exclude from that count the use of small quantities of flour for thickening, oil for greasing and frying, and salt and pepper for seasoning.

MEASUREMENTS

Standard metric cup and spoon measures are used in this book.

1 cup	= 250ml
½ cup	= 125ml
⅓ cup	= 80ml
¼ cup	= 60ml
1 tbsp	= 15ml*
1 tsp	= 5 ml

* Australian readers need to be aware that a standard Australian tablespoon is 20ml, so you will need to use 3 teaspoons wherever I call for 1 tablespoon.

BREAK

&
LUNCH

FAST

Overnight Oats

PREP TIME
5 MINUTES

SOAKING TIME
OVERNIGHT

SERVES
2–3

Overnight oats are the perfect breakfast option for those who have little time in the morning. They are creamy, nourishing, totally delicious and will keep you fuelled all morning. This is a very basic recipe and can be easily adapted to your liking. Optional additions can include berries, chopped nuts, fresh or dried fruit, coconut, cinnamon, vanilla extract — I could go on and on. Otherwise just enjoy it on its own. I sometimes heat it in the microwave just before serving for a warm, comforting winter breakfast. You can use regular milk, but almond, oat, soy or cashew all work.

INGREDIENTS

1 cup (90g) rolled oats

2 tbsp chia seeds

2 cups (500ml) milk, plus extra to serve

1 tbsp pure maple syrup or runny honey

¼ tsp salt

any optional additions you desire

Mix all the ingredients together in a bowl until well combined. Cover, then place in the fridge overnight.

To serve, divide among bowls, drizzle with extra milk and add your choice of topping.

You can make a larger batch and keep in the fridge for up to 3 days.

Breakfast Bake

 PREP TIME
10 MINUTES

 COOKING TIME
45–50 MINUTES

 SERVES
6–8

You can have your own café-style brunch at home with this easy throw together recipe, and of course you can alter it according to your taste and what ingredients you have on hand. You can add chopped onion, mushrooms, capsicum, ham, fresh herbs, spinach — the list can go on. Don't think you can only eat this for breakfast; it's great for picnics, lunch and dinner. You can also prepare the entire dish the night before and leave it covered in the fridge until ready to cook in the morning.

INGREDIENTS

750g mini hash browns

5 rashers bacon, chopped

8 eggs

½ cup (125ml) milk or cream

1 tsp salt

2 cups (240g) grated tasty cheese

chopped herbs, to serve (optional)

Preheat the oven to 180°C. Grease a 23cm × 33cm baking dish.

Arrange the hash browns in a single layer in the baking dish and scatter the chopped bacon over.

Place the eggs, milk or cream and salt in a bowl and season with pepper. Whisk until well combined. Pour over the hash browns and bacon, then sprinkle with grated cheese.

Bake, uncovered, for 45–50 minutes or until set and the cheese is golden. Sprinkle with herbs, if using, and cut into pieces to serve.

Leftovers Fritters

PREP TIME
10 MINUTES

COOKING TIME
8–16 MINUTES

SERVES
2–3

This is a great recipe to have up your sleeve when you have leftovers you don't know what to do with. Throw in any combination of ingredients you have laying about in your fridge to create a meal out of all those bits and pieces. Here are some suggestions — leftover roast meat and roast vegetables, leftover cooked rice or pasta, sliced cooked broccoli, cauliflower, carrots, onions, cooked bacon, ham, spring onions, zucchini, capsicum and/or herbs. You can also use thawed frozen vegetables in your freezer that need consuming. Be as creative as you wish!

INGREDIENTS

2 cups chopped leftovers

2 eggs, lightly beaten

2 tbsp self-raising flour

½ cup (60g) grated tasty cheese

1 tsp curry powder

vegetable oil, for frying

Place all the ingredients in a bowl and mix until well combined. Season with salt and pepper to taste (about ½ tsp of each).

Coat the bottom of a frying pan with oil and place over medium heat. Drop tablespoons of mixture into the pan and shallow-fry for about 4 minutes each side, or until golden and cooked through. You may need to do this in two batches, depending on the size of your pan.

Serve warm, on their own or with your choice of sides.

Healthy Muffins

PREP TIME
10 MINUTES

COOKING TIME
15–20 MINUTES

MAKES
12

I often make a batch of these and keep them in the freezer so I can take one out each morning to take to work. They are free of refined sugar and substantial enough to keep my energy levels up during the day. Feel free to stir through a handful of chocolate chips or berries after processing the other ingredients if desired.

INGREDIENTS

1 cup (140g) pitted dates, chopped

1½ cups (180g) oat bran (see Tip)

3 bananas, chopped

2 eggs

1 tsp bicarb soda

¼ tsp salt

Preheat the oven to 180°C. Line a 12-cup muffin tray with paper cases.

Place the dates into a small bowl and pour over enough boiling water to cover them. Set aside for 5 minutes to soften, then drain well.

Place all the ingredients into a food processor and process until smooth. Divide evenly among the muffin cases.

Bake for 15–20 minutes or until the muffins spring back when pressed lightly. Serve warm or at room temperature.

> **TIP:** If you don't have oat bran you can put 2 cups (180g) rolled oats in the food processor and process until fine.

Vanilla Yoghurt Muffins

PREP TIME
10 MINUTES

COOKING TIME
20 MINUTES

MAKES
12

These basic little muffins are light and soft and can easily be adapted to many other variations. The use of vanilla yoghurt ensures they stay moist and gives them a hint of extra vanilla flavour. If you don't have vanilla yoghurt you can use plain sweetened yoghurt with 1 tsp vanilla extract.

INGREDIENTS

⅓ cup (80ml) runny honey

2 eggs

100g butter, melted

1 cup (280g) vanilla yoghurt

2 cups (300g) self-raising flour

¼ tsp salt

icing sugar, to dust (optional)

Preheat the oven to 180°C. Line a 12-cup muffin tray with paper cases.

Place the honey, eggs, butter and yoghurt in a large bowl and whisk until well combined. Sift the flour and salt into the bowl and mix until just combined. Divide evenly among the muffin cases.

Bake for 20 minutes or until the muffins spring back when pressed lightly. Serve warm or at room temperature, dusted with icing sugar, if using.

> **VARIATIONS:**
> - **To make Banana Muffins**, add 2 mashed bananas to the wet ingredients.
> - **To make Berry Muffins**, gently fold in 1 cup (150g) fresh or frozen berries.
> - **To make Chocolate Chip Muffins**, fold in ½ cup (95g) chocolate chips.

Lunchbox Scrolls

PREP TIME
10 MINUTES

COOKING TIME
20–25 MINUTES

MAKES
12–15

I won't forget the never-ending struggle to find ideas for my children's lunch boxes that were easy, economical, filling and that were going to be eaten. These scrolls were always very popular and the great thing about them is you can fill them with a never-ending array of ingredients. See the variation ideas below.

INGREDIENTS

2 cups (300g) self-raising flour

60g cold butter, grated

¾ cup (180ml) milk

2 tbsp Marmite or Vegemite

2 cups (240g) grated tasty cheese

Preheat the oven to 180°C. Grease a baking tray and line with baking paper.

Sift the flour and a pinch of salt into a large bowl. Add the grated butter and mix until well combined. Stir in the milk with a butter knife until a dough is formed. You may need to add a little extra milk or flour to achieve this.

Turn onto a floured bench and knead lightly until smooth. Roll out to a 40cm × 20cm rectangle. Spread with Marmite or Vegemite and sprinkle the cheese over. Working from a long side, roll up tightly.

Trim the ends and then cut the roll into 12–15 even slices. Place onto the prepared tray, cut-side up and about 1cm apart.

Bake for 20–25 minutes or until golden. Serve warm or cold. Store in an airtight container in the fridge and consume within 2 days. Can be frozen for up to 2 months.

VARIATIONS:

- Ham or bacon and cheese.
- Ham, cheese and pineapple.
- Pesto or fruit chutney and cheese.
- Pizza sauce and cheese.
- BBQ or sweet chilli sauce and chopped cooked chicken.
- Stewed apple, brown sugar and cinnamon.
- Your own fabulous combo!

Almond Maple Cookies

PREP TIME
5 MINUTES

COOKING TIME
12–15 MINUTES

MAKES
12

There are many reasons why you need to make these cookies. They take 5 minutes to prepare, they use only 4 ingredients (one of which is salt), they are vegan, gluten-free, keto-friendly (if you use sugar-free maple-flavoured syrup) and, above all, they are delicious! Their soft, chewy centre makes them very moreish, so be warned! They can also be dipped in dark chocolate if desired.

INGREDIENTS

2 cups (240g) almond flour

¼ cup (60ml) pure maple syrup or sugar-free maple-flavoured syrup

1 tsp vanilla extract

¼ tsp salt

Preheat the oven to 180°C. Grease a baking tray and line with baking paper.

Place all the ingredients into a bowl. Mix until well combined and a dough is formed. Using wet hands, roll the dough into golf ball-sized balls. Place on the prepared tray and flatten the balls with your hands.

Bake for 12–15 minutes or until the edges start to brown. Transfer to a wire rack to cool completely.

Store in an airtight container for up to 1 week either at room temperature or in the fridge, or freeze for up to 1 month.

Caramel Cookies

PREP TIME
10 MINUTES
(+ 15 MINUTES
CHILLING)

COOKING TIME
12–15 MINUTES

MAKES
12

The use of caramel filling instead of condensed milk in this recipe gives these cookies a real depth of flavour which can be a little addictive! For extra decadence you can also add a handful of chocolate chips before adding the flour.

INGREDIENTS

100g butter, melted and cooled

200g (½ 395g tin) caramel filling

¼ cup (55g) brown sugar

1 tsp vanilla extract

1½ cups (225g) self-raising flour

¼ tsp salt

Preheat the oven to 180°C. Grease a baking tray and line with baking paper.

Whisk the butter, caramel filling, brown sugar and vanilla extract in a large bowl until well combined. Sift in the flour and salt, and mix until just combined. Place in the fridge for 15 minutes to firm up.

Roll the dough into golf ball-sized balls and place on the tray, leaving room for the cookies to spread. Flatten slightly with a fork.

Bake for 12–15 minutes or until golden. Transfer to a wire rack to cool completely

Store in an airtight container for up to 1 week, or freeze for up to 3 months.

> **TIP:** Use the other half of the tin of caramel filling to make the Salted Caramel Ice Cream on page 180.

Custard Cookies

The texture of these cookies resembles shortbread due to the use of icing sugar, and the flavour is that of vanilla custard. The combined texture and flavour makes these little cookies so delicious. They are the perfect treat to have with your next cuppa. Oh, and did I mention they are super easy to prepare?

PREP TIME
10 MINUTES

COOKING TIME
15 MINUTES

MAKES
16

INGREDIENTS

200g butter, chopped

1 tsp vanilla extract

½ cup (80g) icing sugar

½ cup (60g) custard powder

1½ cups (225g) self-raising flour

pinch of salt

Preheat the oven to 180°C. Grease a baking tray and line with baking paper.

Heat the butter in a saucepan until just melted, then remove from the heat. Stir in the vanilla extract.

Sift in the remaining ingredients and mix until combined.

Roll the mixture into golf ball-sized balls. Place onto the prepared tray and flatten with a fork.

Bake for 15 minutes or until slightly golden. Transfer to a wire rack to cool completely

Store in an airtight container for up to 1 week, or freeze for up to 3 months.

Ginger Brownies

<u>PREP TIME</u>
10 MINUTES

<u>COOKING TIME</u>
25 MINUTES

<u>MAKES</u>
9

Chocolate brownies would have to be one of the world's most loved baked treats, but here is an alternative — ginger brownies. They still have the same consistency as chocolate brownies, with a soft and chewy interior, but they are made with the warming spice of ginger instead of chocolate or cocoa.

INGREDIENTS

150g butter, melted and cooled

1½ cups (330g) brown sugar

3 eggs

1 cup (150g) plain flour

2 tbsp ground ginger

¼ tsp salt

Preheat the oven to 180°C. Grease a 20cm square cake pan and line with baking paper.

Place the melted butter and sugar in a bowl and whisk until well combined. Whisk in the eggs. Sift in the flour, ginger and salt and fold through to combine. Pour the mixture into the prepared pan.

Bake for 25 minutes, or until the brownie springs back when pressed lightly. Cool in the pan then cut into pieces.

Store in an airtight container for up to 1 week, or freeze for up to 1 month.

VARIATION: If you don't like ginger then try making coffee brownies. Add 1 tbsp instant coffee granules or powder into the melted butter and omit the ground ginger.

Banana Cake

PREP TIME
10 MINUTES

COOKING TIME
30–35 MINUTES

SERVES
12

If you have over-ripe bananas laying around then this recipe is a great way to use them up. It's deliciously moist and always goes down a treat. You can ice, dust with icing sugar or enjoy the cake just as it is. It's also delicious served with a dollop of vanilla yoghurt or whipped cream.

INGREDIENTS

1½ cups (350g) mashed ripe bananas (approx. 3 large bananas)

1 cup (220g) brown sugar

2 eggs

½ cup (125ml) neutral oil (canola, vegetable or grapeseed)

1 tsp vanilla extract (optional)

1½ cups (225g) self-raising flour

icing sugar, to dust (optional)

Preheat the oven to 180°C. Grease a 23cm round cake pan and line with baking paper.

Place the bananas, sugar, eggs, oil and vanilla (if using) in a bowl and whisk until well combined. Sift in the flour and gently mix until just combined. Be careful not to overmix as this could make the cake dense. Pour the mixture into the prepared pan and spread out evenly.

Bake for 30–35 minutes, or until a skewer inserted into the centre comes out clean and the cake is golden brown on top. Cool in the pan for 10 minutes then transfer to a wire rack to cool completely. Dust with icing sugar to serve, if using.

Store in an airtight container for up to 1 week, or freeze for up to 3 months.

Golden Sultana Loaf

PREP TIME
10 MINUTES

COOKING TIME
40 MINUTES

SERVES
10

I've discovered recently that people either love or hate sultanas, which I find fascinating as I have always loved anything sultana. If you are a lover of sultanas, then you must give this recipe a go. It tastes great freshly baked, but becomes even more delicious after a couple of days.

INGREDIENTS

1 cup (250ml) cream

2 tbsp golden syrup

1 tsp vanilla extract (optional)

2 cups (300g) self-raising flour

½ cup (110g) white sugar

1 cup (80g) sultanas

Preheat the oven to 180°C. Grease a loaf pan and line with baking paper.

Warm the cream in a small saucepan then add the golden syrup and mix until dissolved. Stir in the vanilla if using.

Sift the flour and sugar into a bowl then stir in the sultanas. Pour in the cream mixture and mix until just combined. Tip the mixture into the prepared pan and spread out evenly.

Bake for 40 minutes or until a skewer inserted into the centre comes out clean. Cool in the pan, then lift out and cut into slices to serve.

Store in an airtight container for up to 1 week, or freeze either whole or sliced and wrapped for up to 3 months.

Blueberry Loaf

The use of cream in this recipe ensures the loaf remains deliciously moist. It is the perfect morning- or afternoon-tea treat, especially with a spread of butter! Feel free to add 1 tsp finely grated lemon rind or vanilla extract for extra flavour if desired, but it is delicious just as it is.

PREP TIME
10 MINUTES

COOKING TIME
40–50 MINUTES

SERVES
10

INGREDIENTS

2 cups (300g) self-raising flour

1 cup (220g) white sugar

¼ tsp salt

1 cup (150g) fresh or frozen blueberries

1 cup (250ml) cream

2 eggs

icing sugar, to dust (optional)

Preheat the oven to 180°C. Grease a loaf pan and line with baking paper.

Sift the flour, sugar and salt into a bowl, then add the blueberries. Mix until combined. In another bowl, whisk the cream and eggs until well combined. Pour the wet mixture into the dry mixture and mix until just combined. Be careful not to overmix, as it may result in a dense loaf. Tip the mixture into the prepared pan, spreading it out evenly.

Bake for 40–50 minutes or until a skewer inserted into the centre comes out clean. Allow the loaf to cool for 10 minutes then transfer to a wire rack to cool completely. Dust with icing sugar, and serve spread with butter if you like.

Store in an airtight container for up to 1 week or freeze for up to 1 month.

Cream Scones

PREP TIME
10 MINUTES

COOKING TIME
12–15 MINUTES

MAKES
8

If you're anything like me and don't enjoy the process of rubbing butter into flour when making scones, then try this recipe. The use of cream gives these scones enough fat to omit the butter. The results are light, fluffy scones begging to be devoured with your favourite jam and whipped cream slathered on top. Feel free to add a cup or so of sultanas or chopped dates. It's also delicious to add the finely grated rind of an orange for an orange-flavoured scone.

INGREDIENTS

1 egg

2 tbsp white sugar

½ cup (125ml) cream

½ cup (125ml) milk, plus extra to brush

2 cups (300g) self-raising flour

¼ tsp salt

jam and cream, to serve

icing sugar, to dust (optional)

Preheat the oven to 220°C. Grease a baking tray.

Place the egg and sugar in a mixing bowl. Use electric beaters to beat for about 2 minutes, until light and creamy.

Add the cream and milk and beat until well combined. Sift in the flour and salt and gently mix with a knife until just combined, adding a little extra flour if needed.

Turn onto a floured bench and shape into a 3cm thick rectangle. Gently cut into 8 pieces, using a knife or scone cutter. Place scones onto the prepared tray, making sure they are close together but with a little space between each one.

Brush the tops with a little milk and bake for 12–15 minutes or until well risen and lightly golden.

Cool and serve with jam and cream. Dust lightly with icing sugar if you like.

Healthy Apricot and Coconut Balls

These little balls are full of flavour and a great pick-me-up when you're after a healthy, sweet treat. The milk powder gives them a creamy texture.

 PREP TIME
10 MINUTES

 COOKING TIME
0 MINUTES

 MAKES
12

INGREDIENTS

1 cup (150g) chopped dried apricots

½ cup (40g) desiccated coconut

½ cup (50g) milk powder

¼ cup (30g) oat bran
(see Tip)

2 tbsp boiling water

extra desiccated coconut for rolling (optional)

Place all the ingredients into a food processor and process until well combined. Form the mixture into 12 balls. Roll the balls into extra coconut if desired.

Store in an airtight container in the fridge and consume within 2 weeks.

> **TIP:** If you don't have oat bran you can put ½ cup (45g) rolled oats in the food processor and process until fine, then add the other ingredients.

Peanut Butter Muesli Bars

This recipe lets you customise your muesli bars by using your favourite ingredients, or whatever you happen to have on hand. If you can't tolerate peanuts then you can use any other nut butter.

PREP TIME
10 MINUTES

COOKING TIME
20–25 MINUTES

MAKES
16

INGREDIENTS

½ cup (125ml) runny honey

½ cup (140g) peanut butter

2 cups (180g) rolled oats

1 cup (100g–150g) chopped nuts and/or seeds (walnuts, almonds, sunflower seeds, pumpkin seeds)

1 cup (150g) dried fruit (raisins, cranberries or chopped dates or apricots)

Preheat the oven to 180°C. Grease a 20cm × 30cm slice pan and line with baking paper.

Place the honey and peanut butter in a large microwave-safe bowl. Microwave until melted, then stir to combine. Add the remaining ingredients and mix until well combined. Tip the mixture into the prepared pan and press down firmly to make an even layer (this prevents the bars from being crumbly).

Bake for 20–25 minutes, or until the edges are golden brown. Set aside to cool, then cut into bars.

Store in an airtight container at room temperature for up to 1 week or freeze for up to 1 month.

Lemon Squares

If you love all things lemon, then I am sure this recipe will become a favourite. It has a crunchy base and a creamy, lemony filling. Simple but very delicious!

PREP TIME
10 MINUTES

COOKING TIME
15 MINUTES (+ 3 HOURS CHILLING)

MAKES
12

INGREDIENTS

250g pkt plain sweet biscuits, crushed

140g butter, melted and cooled

395g tin sweetened condensed milk

1 tsp finely grated lemon rind

½ cup (125ml) lemon juice

4 eggs

TIP: A typical lemon provides about 2–3 tbsp lemon juice. It's also much easier to grate and shred the rind before you juice your lemons.

Preheat the oven to 180°C. Grease a 20cm × 30cm slice pan and line with baking paper.

Place the crushed biscuits and melted butter into a bowl and mix until well combined. Press into the prepared pan in an even layer. Refrigerate while you prepare the filling.

Combine the condensed milk, lemon rind, juice and eggs in a bowl. Beat with electric beaters for about 2 minutes, until creamy (it is quite a runny mixture). Pour over the biscuit base.

Bake for 15 minutes or until the centre is set. Cool, then place in the fridge for at least 3 hours to chill.

Cut into squares to serve.

Store in an airtight container in the fridge for up to 1 week.

No-bake Chocolate Cornflake Slice

PREP TIME
10 MINUTES

SETTING TIME
2 HOURS

SERVES
16

This chocolatey, crunchy, sweet treat can be whipped up within minutes and requires no baking. It is very popular in my household and never lasts long.

INGREDIENTS

1 cup (250g) coconut oil

3 cups (120g) Cornflakes

3 tbsp cocoa powder

1 cup (160g) icing sugar

1 cup (150g) raisins or sultanas

Grease a 20cm square baking dish or cake pan. Melt the coconut oil in a large saucepan. Remove from the heat and add the remaining ingredients. Mix until well combined.

Tip the mixture into the prepared dish and distribute evenly. Place in the fridge for about 2 hours, until set. Cut into desired sized portions and watch them go!

Store in an airtight container in the fridge for up to 1 week.

Versatile Five-cup Slice

PREP TIME
10 MINUTES

COOKING TIME
12–15 MINUTES

SERVES
12

What this slice lacks in visual appeal it certainly makes up in total deliciousness. It's a very versatile recipe as you can use whatever ingredients you have on hand. If you want to leave out the chocolate, make up the volume with extra cereal, fruit, or nuts and seeds. Either way, it is sure to be a big hit!

INGREDIENTS

395g tin sweetened condensed milk

1 cup (40g–90g) cereal (Rice Bubbles, Cornflakes, rolled oats or muesli)

1 cup (150g) dried fruit (chopped dates, chopped apricots, sultanas, raisins, cranberries)

1 cup (100g–150g) chopped nuts or seeds (peanuts, cashews, walnuts, almonds, sunflower seeds, pumpkin seeds)

1 cup (190g) chocolate chips (milk, dark and/or white)

Preheat the oven to 180°C. Grease a 20cm × 30cm slice pan and line with baking paper.

Place all the ingredients into a large bowl and mix until well combined. Using damp hands, press the mixture into the prepared pan to make an even layer.

Bake for 12–15 minutes or until golden and bubbly. Allow to cool slightly in the pan for 10 minutes before transferring to a wire rack to cool completely. Cut into desired sizes.

Store in an airtight container in the fridge for up to 1 week or freeze for up to 6 weeks.

Walnut Slice

PREP TIME
10 MINUTES

COOKING TIME
20 MINUTES

SERVES
9

INGREDIENTS

1 cup (150g) self-raising flour

½ cup (110g) brown sugar

½ cup (40g) desiccated coconut

½ cup (55g) chopped walnuts

120g butter, melted and cooled

This is such an easy recipe to whip up and is easily adapted if you don't have walnuts on hand. The walnuts can be replaced with any type of nuts or dried fruit.

Preheat the oven to 180°C. Grease a 20cm square cake pan and line with baking paper.

Place the dry ingredients into a bowl and mix until evenly combined. Make a well in the centre and pour in the melted butter. Mix until well combined. Tip the mixture into the prepared pan and press out to an even layer.

Bake for 20 minutes or until golden brown. Cool in the pan then cut into squares.

Store in an airtight container at room temperature for up to 1 week, or freeze for up to 2 months.

MAINS

French Onion Soup

PREP TIME
15 MINUTES

COOKING TIME
35–40 MINUTES

SERVES
4

French onion soup was a staple back in the 1970s but unfortunately has all but disappeared. It's a shame, because onions are so readily available and always economical to purchase. This is a very basic version and delicious just as it is; however, you can also add a little thyme, a tablespoon of Worcestershire sauce, a splash of white wine, or a bay leaf when adding the stock for extra flavour. Just remember to remove the bay leaf before serving. It's a full-bodied, hearty soup, perfect to warm you up on a cold winter's day.

INGREDIENTS

3 tbsp vegetable oil

6 large onions, halved and thinly sliced

4 garlic cloves, crushed

2 tbsp plain flour

4 cups (1 litre) beef stock

8 slices French baguette

½ cup (120g) grated gruyere or tasty cheese

chopped parsley, to serve (optional)

Heat the oil in a large saucepan on medium heat. Add the onion and garlic and cook, stirring occasionally, for 15–20 minutes or until soft and brown.

Sprinkle the flour over and cook, stirring, for 1 minute. Gradually add the stock, stirring to combine. Bring just to the boil. Cover, reduce the heat slightly and gently simmer for 20 minutes.

While the soup is cooking, lightly toast the baguette slices. Place the cheese on top and grill until the cheese has melted. Season the soup with salt and plenty of pepper, to taste.

Serve soup topped with the toasted baguette slices, and sprinkled with parsley if using.

Japanese-inspired Baked Salmon

We are constantly being told of the importance of including fish in our diets, and with this recipe it couldn't be easier. I love how this sauce is salty, tart and sweet, with the warmth of ginger. A simply delicious option for a mid-week dinner or dinner party.

PREP TIME
5 MINUTES
(+ 2 HOURS
MARINATING TIME
AND COOLING)

COOKING TIME
20–25 MINUTES

SERVES
4

INGREDIENTS

4 pieces boneless salmon fillet, about 150g each

chopped parsley or coriander, to serve (optional)

SOY MARINADE

¼ cup (60ml) soy sauce

¼ cup (60ml) rice wine vinegar

2 tbsp brown sugar

2 tbsp minced ginger

Place the soy marinade ingredients into a small saucepan and bring to a simmer over medium-low heat. Cook gently for 5 minutes, then transfer to a bowl or jug to cool.

Place the salmon, skin side down, into a lightly oiled baking dish. Pour over the marinade then cover and place in the fridge to marinate for at least 2 hours, or up to 12 hours.

Preheat the oven to 200°C. Cover the baking dish with foil and bake the salmon for 15–20 minutes or until cooked through and flaky.

Serve drizzled with any sauce remaining in the tray, and sprinkle with herbs, if using.

Bacon-wrapped Chicken

PREP TIME
10 MINUTES

COOKING TIME
35–40 MINUTES

SERVES
4

Wrapping chicken in bacon not only adds flavour but also ensures the chicken remains moist and juicy. Topped with a sweet BBQ glaze, these little bundles of joy are sure to be a hit at your next dinner party or mid-week family gathering. You can also cook these in your air fryer or on a rack on the BBQ with the lid down, although you may need to alter the cooking time.

INGREDIENTS

1kg skinless, boneless chicken thighs

4–8 rashers streaky bacon

¼ cup (60ml) BBQ sauce

1 tbsp brown sugar

1 tsp mustard powder

small coriander leaves, to serve (optional)

Preheat the oven to 180°C. Grease a baking tray and line with baking paper. Season the chicken with salt and pepper. Wrap each thigh with a rasher or two of bacon, ensuring the ends are tucked underneath the chicken or secured with a toothpick. Place onto the prepared tray.

In a small bowl, mix the BBQ sauce, sugar and mustard powder until well combined. Brush half the glaze mixture over the bacon-wrapped chicken.

Bake for 20 minutes then brush the chicken with the remaining glaze mixture. Bake for an additional 15–20 minutes or until the chicken is cooked through and the glaze is bubbling.

Serve sprinkled with coriander, if using.

Creamy Chicken and Mushrooms

PREP TIME
10 MINUTES

COOKING TIME
15 MINUTES

SERVES
4

This quick and easy recipe is a firm mid-week favourite in our household. I like to serve it with creamy mashed potatoes and steamed vegetables to soak up the luscious sauce. It's also delicious served over rice or noodles. Don't go easy on the pepper as this will heighten the flavour of the mushrooms.

INGREDIENTS

vegetable oil, for frying

700g skinless, boneless chicken breasts or thighs, cut into 2cm cubes

300g mushrooms, sliced

1 onion, finely chopped

3 tbsp Worcestershire sauce

½ cup (125ml) cream

chopped parsley, to serve (optional)

Lightly coat the bottom of a large frying pan with oil and heat over high heat. Season the chicken with salt and pepper then add to the frying pan. Stir-fry for 6–8 minutes, until the chicken is just cooked through. Transfer the chicken to a plate, and set aside.

Add a little more oil to the frying pan and add the mushrooms and onion. Stir-fry for 5–6 minutes or until soft and golden. Add the chicken back to the frying pan along with the Worcestershire sauce and cream. Cook, stirring, for 1–2 minutes or until the sauce thickens.

Season with salt and plenty of pepper, to taste. Serve immediately, sprinkled with parsley if using.

Lemon, Basil and Feta Chicken

PREP TIME
10 MINUTES

COOKING TIME
20–25 MINUTES

SERVES
4

The combination of these simple Mediterranean flavours will have your taste buds singing. Such an easy way to jazz up chicken breasts and have you looking like a culinary genius at the same time. You can use chicken breasts or thighs in this recipe.

INGREDIENTS

2 tbsp olive oil

2 tbsp lemon juice

4 skinless, boneless chicken breasts or thighs

2 tbsp finely shredded lemon rind

⅓ cup roughly chopped basil leaves

120g feta, crumbled

salad, to serve

Preheat the oven to 200°C.

Combine the oil and lemon juice in an ovenproof dish that will fit the chicken snugly but with a little gap between each piece. Add the chicken and turn to coat in the marinade. Sprinkle the top of the chicken with the lemon rind, basil and feta. Season with freshly ground black pepper.

Bake for 20–25 minutes or until topping is golden brown and chicken is cooked through. Cover with foil during cooking if the topping starts to burn.

Rest for 5 minutes before serving with salad.

Baked Chicken Curry

I love adapting recipes that usually require lots of frying and stirring over the stovetop, to ones that are baked. The oven does all the hard work for you and saves a lot of hands-on time. This baked chicken curry is one of those recipes. You can use any cut of chicken in this recipe as long as the pieces have their skin on and bone in.

PREP TIME
10 MINUTES

COOKING TIME
45–50 MINUTES

SERVES
4

INGREDIENTS

6–8 skin-on, bone-in chicken pieces (such as thighs and drumsticks)

vegetable oil

1–2 tbsp red curry paste (more or less depending on your taste)

1½ cups (375ml) coconut milk

1 tsp fish sauce

1 tsp white sugar

rice, yoghurt and chopped coriander, to serve (optional)

Preheat the oven to 180°C. Grease a roasting dish which is just big enough to fit the chicken in a single layer with a little gap between each piece.

Rub a small amount of oil on the chicken pieces and season with salt and pepper. Place into the prepared dish. Combine the remaining ingredients in a jug and mix until well combined. Pour over the chicken.

Bake uncovered for 45–50 minutes or until the chicken is cooked through and the skin is golden.

Transfer the chicken to a serving platter and pour over the sauce. Serve with rice and yoghurt, sprinkled with coriander, if using.

Slow Cooker Honey-Garlic Chicken

PREP TIME
5 MINUTES

COOKING TIME
2–3 OR 4–5 HOURS

SERVES
4

INGREDIENTS

6–8 skinless, bone-in chicken thighs

⅓ cup (80ml) runny honey

¼ cup (60ml) BBQ sauce or tomato sauce

¼ cup (60ml) salt-reduced soy sauce

6 garlic cloves, crushed

1 tbsp cornflour (optional)

rice or mashed potatoes, and chopped parsley or coriander, to serve (optional)

If you think you don't have time to cook then think again. This recipe literally takes 5 minutes to prepare, at which point your slow cooker will take over. In a few hours (while you go and do other things), it will present you with a tasty meal your family is going to rave about. The chicken is so tender it will almost fall off the bone and any leftover sauce will be lapped up. Serve with rice or mashed potatoes.

Place the chicken into a slow cooker. Place the remaining ingredients (except the cornflour) in a jug with ¼ cup (60ml) water and whisk to combine. Pour over the chicken.

Cover and cook on high for 2–3 hours or low for 4–5 hours, until the chicken is very tender. If you would like to thicken the sauce, mix the cornflour with a little water then mix in with the chicken about 20 minutes before the end of the cooking time.

Serve with rice or mashed potatoes, and chopped herbs, if using.

> **TIP:** It is best to use skinless chicken thighs in this recipe. However, if you use skin-on chicken thighs, you will need to sear the chicken, skin down, in a frying pan to render some of the fat and brown the skin.

Mains

○●○○

Slow Cooker Moroccan Apricot Chicken

PREP TIME
5 MINUTES

COOKING TIME
4 HOURS OR
7–8 HOURS

SERVES
4

It only takes a few minutes to prepare this recipe. Using store-bought Moroccan seasoning cuts down on having to use an array of other spices and adds that little bit of heat without it being overpowering. Add to that the sweet tanginess of the apricots and honey and your taste buds are going to be in for a treat

INGREDIENTS

1kg skinless, boneless chicken thighs

410g tin apricot halves

½ pkt (30g) dried French onion soup mix

2 tbsp Moroccan seasoning

1 tbsp runny honey

chopped mint, to serve (optional)

rice or couscous, to serve

Place the chicken into a slow cooker. Drain the apricots and reserve the juice. Add the drained apricots to the slow cooker.

Add enough water to the reserved juice to make up 1 cup (250ml) liquid. Add the soup mix, Moroccan seasoning and honey and whisk until well combined. Pour over the chicken and apricots.

Cover and cook for on high for 4 hours or low for 7–8 hours, until the chicken is very tender.

Sprinkle with mint, if using, and serve with rice or couscous.

Sweet and Sour Chicken

PREP TIME
5 MINUTES

COOKING TIME
10 MINUTES

SERVES
4

If you would like to have dinner on the table within 15 minutes, then try out this classic dish. It uses minimal ingredients that you've probably already got in your pantry and, unlike other sweet and sour sauces, does not contain pineapple. Serve with your favourite veggies.

INGREDIENTS

700g skinless, boneless chicken thighs or breasts

1 tbsp vegetable oil

⅓ cup (75g) brown sugar

1 tbsp cornflour

¼ cup (60ml) tomato sauce

2 tbsp white wine vinegar or rice vinegar

rice and coriander, to serve (optional)

Cut the chicken into bite-sized pieces.

Heat the oil in a large frying pan on high heat. Cook the chicken for about 8 minutes, turning and stirring occasionally, until cooked through.

Combine the remaining ingredients in a jug with ½ cup (125ml) water and mix until well combined. Pour the sauce over the chicken and cook, stirring, for a minute or two until the sauce has thickened and is heated through.

Serve with rice, and sprinkle with coriander if using.

Tuscan Yoghurt-marinated Chicken

PREP TIME
10 MINUTES (+ 30 MINUTES–3 HOURS MARINATING)

COOKING TIME
20 OR 30 MINUTES, DEPENDING ON COOKING METHOD

SERVES
4

If you've never marinated chicken in yoghurt before then you're missing a treat. The lactic acid in the yoghurt naturally tenderises the chicken, leaving it tangy and juicy. You can use any cut of chicken in this recipe but my favourite is boneless thighs, either with or without the skin. You can cook this any number of ways including on the BBQ or in the oven, and it's fabulous cooked in the air fryer. Serve with any favourite veggie accompaniment.

INGREDIENTS

½ cup (140g) plain Greek yoghurt

1 tbsp finely grated lemon rind

¼ cup (60ml) lemon juice

2 tbsp Tuscan or Italian seasoning

3 tsp minced garlic

700g skinless, boneless chicken thighs

shredded lemon rind, to serve (optional)

Place the yoghurt, grated lemon rind, juice, seasoning and garlic in a large bowl and mix to combine. Add the chicken and stir coat. Cover and marinate for at least 30 minutes, or in the fridge for up to 3 hours. If marinating for the longer time, remove from the fridge 30 minutes before cooking.

Baking in the oven – preheat the oven to 200°C and grease a baking tray. Place chicken on the tray, leaving a gap between each piece, and season with salt and pepper. Bake for 30 minutes or until cooked through, turning halfway through cooking.

Cooking on the BBQ – heat BBQ to medium and brush the grill plates with oil. Place chicken on the grill and season with salt and pepper. Cook for 8–10 minutes each side or until cooked through.

Cooking in the air fryer – preheat air fryer to 180°C. Place chicken in the air fryer basket in a single layer and season with salt and pepper. Bake for 20 minutes or until cooked through, turning halfway through cooking.

Sprinkle with shredded lemon rind to serve.

Beef Casserole

PREP TIME
10 MINUTES

COOKING TIME
2 HOURS

SERVES
4

The combination of tomato, pineapple and beef may seem a little unusual, but believe me it's delicious. So easy to throw together for a hearty mid-week dinner. It is great served with mashed potatoes, rice or crusty bread, and steamed vegetables.

INGREDIENTS

800g stewing beef, cut into 2cm cubes

1 onion, finely chopped

227g tin pineapple chunks, including juice

45g pkt dried tomato soup mix

3 tbsp soy sauce

mashed potatoes, rice and/or crusty bread, to serve

chopped parsley, to serve (optional)

Preheat the oven to 180°C.

Place all the ingredients into a casserole dish and add 1 cup (250ml) water. Season with salt and plenty of pepper and stir until well combined.

Cover and bake for 2 hours, stirring occasionally.

Serve with rice and/or bread, sprinkled with parsley, if using.

Meatloaf

PREP TIME
10 MINUTES

COOKING TIME
50–60 MINUTES

SERVES
4

This may be a basic meatloaf recipe, but it still packs a lot of flavour. You can easily adapt this by using tomato relish instead of sauce or adding mixed herbs, curry powder, garlic or anything else you think will work. It is also delicious adding a layer of grated cheese through the middle, or sprinkled on top about 20 minutes before the end of cooking. You can also use chicken, turkey or lamb mince instead of beef, if you like.

INGREDIENTS

500g beef mince

1 onion, finely chopped

¾ cup (75g) dry breadcrumbs

½ cup (125ml) BBQ sauce or tomato sauce

1 egg

½ tsp each salt and pepper

chopped parsley, to serve

Preheat the oven to 180°C. Grease a baking tray and line with baking paper.

Place all the ingredients into a large bowl. Mix until well combined – your hands are the best tool for this job.

Tip the mixture out onto a board and form into a loaf shape. Place onto the prepared tray.

Bake for 50–60 minutes, until golden brown and cooked through (after inserting a knife into the centre, the juices run clear). Serve sprinkled with parsley, if using.

> **TIP:** Brush the top of the meatloaf with extra BBQ sauce or tomato sauce 5 minutes before end of cooking for a delicious glaze.

Baked Sticky Meatballs

PREP TIME
10 MINUTES

COOKING TIME
45 MINUTES

SERVES
4

INGREDIENTS

500g lean beef mince

½ cup (50g) dried breadcrumbs

½ tsp each salt and pepper

spaghetti and chopped parsley, to serve (optional

STICKY SAUCE

¾ cup (185ml) tomato sauce

3 tbsp brown sugar

2 tbsp Worcestershire sauce

I used to think meatballs needed lots of ingredients to be tasty. Well, I stand corrected. Keeping the meatballs as plain as possible makes the sauce stand out as it's not having to compete with other flavours. The sauce has the perfect balance of savoury and sweet, and if you would like to heat it up then feel free to add some chilli flakes. You could serve these with rice or mashed potatoes instead of spaghetti, if you like. Simple but so delicious.

Preheat the oven to 180°C. Grease a 23cm square baking dish.

Place the sauce ingredients in the prepared dish with ¾ cup (180ml) water and mix until well combined.

Place the mince, breadcrumbs, and salt and pepper in a bowl and mix with your hands until well combined. Shape into golf ball-sized balls and place on top of the sauce. Spoon the sauce over the meatballs.

Bake for 45 minutes, turning the meatballs halfway through cooking.

Serve over spaghetti, and sprinkle with parsley if using.

Slow Cooker Beef Stew

PREP TIME
10 MINUTES

COOKING TIME
8–10 HOURS

SERVES
4

Is there anything more comforting than coming home after a hard day's work to the smell of dinner cooking? The great thing about this recipe is the longer it's left the more tender the meat becomes. So, whether it's cooking for 8 or 10 hours, it doesn't matter — perfect for long days away from home. You can use any cheap cut of beef, as the slow cooking makes the meat so tender it almost melts in your mouth. I often add thawed frozen vegetables half an hour before serving to make it a one-pot wonder. Otherwise, just serve some steamed veggies on the side.

INGREDIENTS

800g stewing beef, cut into 2cm cubes

¼ cup (35g) plain flour

1 tsp each salt and pepper

3 large potatoes, peeled and cut into eighths

1 cup (320g) tomato relish

1 cup (250ml) beef stock

thawed frozen vegetables (optional)

chopped parsley, to serve (optional)

Place the beef, flour, salt and pepper in a large plastic bag and shake well, until the flour coats the beef. Place the beef into the slow cooker and shake over any excess flour.

Add the potatoes and stir to combine with the beef. Mix the relish and stock in a jug then pour over the meat and potatoes. Stir gently to combine.

Cover and cook on low for 8–10 hours. Add thawed vegetables 30 minutes before serving, if using.

Serve sprinkled with parsley, if using.

Parmesan and Mustard Lamb Chops

PREP TIME
10 MINUTES

COOKING TIME
35–45 MINUTES

SERVES
4

Parmesan, mustard and lamb is a combination of flavours made in heaven. Add to this the crunch of the crust and a tender, moist centre, and you've found the perfect way to serve lamb chops. You can also replace the mustard with basil pesto, which is equally delicious.

INGREDIENTS

1 egg

2 tbsp Dijon mustard

2 tbsp cornflour

1 cup (75g) panko breadcrumbs

½ cup (40g) finely grated parmesan

4 lamb shoulder chops or 8 loin chops

salad, crusty bread and chopped parsley, to serve (optional)

Preheat the oven to 180°C. Grease a baking tray.

Whisk the egg, mustard and cornflour in a shallow dish until well combined. Combine the breadcrumbs and cheese in another shallow dish.

Working one at a time, dip a chop into the egg mixture, then coat in the breadcrumbs. Place onto the prepared tray.

Bake for 35–45 minutes, turning halfway through, until cooked through, golden and crispy.

Serve with salad and crusty bread, sprinkled with parsley if using.

Sticky Glazed Lamb Chops

Salty, sweet and sticky — what's not to love about these lamb chops? A delicious mid-week dinner. I love these with the Couscous, Pea and Feta salad on page 133.

PREP TIME
5 MINUTES (+20 MINUTES–8 HOURS MARINATING)

COOKING TIME
40 MINUTES

SERVES
4

INGREDIENTS

4 lamb shoulder chops or 8 loin chops

¼ cup (60ml) soy sauce

¼ cup (60ml) runny honey

2 tbsp Dijon mustard

2 tsp minced garlic

Score the fat on the chops then arrange in a large dish in a single layer. Place the soy sauce, honey, mustard and garlic in a small bowl and mix until well combined. Pour over the chops, ensuring they are covered with the marinade on both sides.

Let the chops marinate for at least 20 minutes at room temperature, or up to 8 hours, covered, in the refrigerator. If marinating in the fridge, take out 20 minutes before cooking.

Preheat the oven to 180°C. Line a baking tray with baking paper (this helps with clean-up).

Place the chops on the tray and season well with salt and pepper on both sides. Reserve remaining marinade.

Bake for 20 minutes then turn over and brush with reserved marinade. Cook for another 20 minutes, or until the chops are sticky and caramelised. Allow to rest for 5 minutes before serving.

Pork Rissoles

PREP TIME
5 MINUTES

COOKING TIME
12–16 MINUTES

SERVES
4

A lady who purchased my books off me at a market a while back gave me this recipe. I'm sorry I did not get her name so I can't credit her. The original recipe was for a meatloaf, which you can still use the mixture for. However, I now use it to make rissoles as the cooking time is much quicker. You can also use the mixture to make cocktail meatballs. Such a handy recipe to have.

INGREDIENTS

500g pork mince

2 × 120g tins baby food apple puree

1 cup (115g) sage and onion stuffing mix

½ tsp each salt and pepper

vegetable oil, for frying

salad, crusty bread and chopped parsley, to serve (optional)

Place all the ingredients, except the oil, in a large bowl and mix to combine. Using wet hands, shape into 10–12 rissoles, about 2cm thick.

Heat the oil in a frying pan over medium heat. Fry the rissoles for 3–4 minutes each side or until cooked through and golden brown. You will need to do this in 2 batches so you don't overcrowd the pan.

Serve with salad and bread, and sprinkle with parsley if using.

Mains

Sausage Pie

PREP TIME
15 MINUTES

COOKING TIME
50-60 MINUTES

SERVES
6

This pie is the perfect dish to take to your next picnic as it's so easy to throw together and transport. It also makes the perfect summer lunch or dinner option when served with a simple salad. As with any sausage recipe, try to buy good quality sausages from your local butcher. The sausage mixture can also be used for making sausage rolls.

INGREDIENTS

3 sheets frozen puff pastry, just thawed

800g beef sausages (about 9 sausages)

1 large onion, grated

½ cup (160g) relish or chutney

1 tsp curry powder

lightly beaten egg or milk for brushing pastry (optional)

Preheat the oven to 180°C. Grease a 20cm × 30cm baking dish and line with baking paper.

Line the prepared dish with a layer of pastry, making sure it comes up the sides of the dish. You will need to use about 1½ sheets of pastry, which you can press together with your fingers at the seam.

Squeeze the sausage meat out of their casings and place into a large bowl along with the onion, relish or chutney and curry powder. Mix with your hands until the ingredients are well combined. Transfer the sausage mixture into the pastry-lined dish and spread out evenly.

Cut the remaining pastry into thin strips and make a lattice pattern on top of the pie. Brush pastry with a little beaten egg or milk if desired.

Bake for 50–60 minutes or until the pastry is golden brown and the centre is cooked through.

Serve warm, or cool to room temperature, cover, and place in the fridge until ready to serve. It will keep in the fridge for up to 2 days.

Macaroni and Cheese

This recipe uses the easiest cheese sauce you'll ever make, no lumps possible! It's a very basic macaroni and cheese so feel free to add extras like cooked bacon, cooked onion and ham. You can also add a teaspoon or two of Dijon mustard to the sauce for extra flavour.

PREP TIME
10 MINUTES

COOKING TIME
30 MINUTES

SERVES
4

INGREDIENTS

2 cups (240g) macaroni, penne or any other small pasta shape

2 cups (500ml) milk

2 tbsp cornflour

2 cups (240g) grated tasty cheese, plus extra to sprinkle

chopped parsley, to serve (optional)

Preheat the oven to 180°C. Grease a 20cm square baking dish.

Cook the pasta in a large pot of salted water until just al dente. Drain well then return the pasta to the pot.

In the meantime, pour the milk into a saucepan, reserving ½ cup. Whisk the cornflour and reserved milk together until smooth. Add to the milk in the saucepan. Bring to the boil over medium heat, stirring until the mixture thickens. Remove from the heat and stir in the cheese until melted. Season with salt and pepper to taste.

Pour the sauce over the pasta and fold through until well combined. Transfer to the prepared baking dish and sprinkle over the extra cheese.

Bake for 20 minutes or until the top is golden and bubbly. Serve sprinkled with parsley if using.

Baked Prawn and Lemon Risoni

PREP TIME
5 MINUTES

COOKING TIME
20 MINUTES

SERVES
2–3

I always keep a bag of prawns in my freezer as they are economical and convenient. Risoni, also known as orzo, is a rice-shaped pasta that is readily available in all supermarkets. This is another staple pantry item I like to keep on hand. With these two items in constant stock, I know I can cook a hearty, delicious meal like this one at any time.

INGREDIENTS

1 cup (220g) risoni

2 tsp chicken stock powder

1 tsp finely grated lemon rind

3 tbsp lemon juice

1½ cups (375ml) boiling water

400g raw peeled prawns (fresh or thawed)

chopped parsley, to taste

shredded lemon rind, to serve (optional)

Preheat oven to 180°C.

Place the risoni, chicken stock powder, grated lemon rind, juice and boiling water in a large casserole dish and mix to combine. Cover tightly with a lid or foil and bake for 10 minutes.

Remove from the oven and stir through the prawns. Cover again and cook for a further 10 minutes or until the risoni is soft and the prawns are cooked through.

Season with salt and pepper and stir through the chopped parsley. Sprinkle with shredded lemon rind, and serve immediately.

Baked Pumpkin Risotto

PREP TIME
10 MINUTES

COOKING TIME
40 MINUTES

SERVES
4

The best thing about this risotto is that it is cooked in the oven, so there is no constant stirring over the stove. The most consuming part of this recipe is grating the pumpkin, but after that it's thrown together in a matter of minutes. If you make this in autumn, when pumpkins are at their best and cheapest, it makes a very economical dinner. I sometimes add 2 cups chopped spinach leaves or a cup of peas (thawed from frozen) at the end of cooking, when you stir in the parmesan. Occasionally I add 1 tbsp fresh or 1 tsp dried sage before cooking to add extra flavour.

INGREDIENTS

400g peeled, deseeded pumpkin, grated

¾ cup (150g) arborio rice

2 tsp vegetable or chicken stock powder

2 tbsp butter

3 cups (750ml) boiling water

1 cup (80g) finely grated parmesan, plus extra to serve

chopped parsley, to serve (optional)

Preheat the oven to 180°C. Grease a 23cm round or square casserole dish.

Place the pumpkin, rice, stock powder, butter and water in the dish and stir to combine. Cover tightly with a lid or foil.

Bake for 40 minutes, or until rice is just tender, stirring halfway through cooking time. Stir through the parmesan and season with plenty of pepper to taste.

Serve topped with extra parmesan, and parsley if using.

> **TIP:** Don't rinse arborio rice as it will strip it of its starch, which is necessary to add creaminess to risotto.

Ravioli Lasagne

I try to make most of my meals from scratch, however, there are times when having a few convenience ingredients on hand saves me from the temptation of dialling for takeaways. This recipe makes use of those ingredients. If I do have extra time up my sleeve, I make my own tomato soup but otherwise it's store-bought. You could swap out the tomato soup for pasta sauce. It's also delicious adding cooked spinach between the layers for extra flavour and goodness.

PREP TIME
10 MINUTES

COOKING TIME
50 MINUTES

SERVES
4

INGREDIENTS

2 cups (500ml) milk

2 tbsp cornflour

1 cup (120g) grated tasty cheese, plus extra to sprinkle

2 cups (500ml) good-quality tomato soup

300g pkt ravioli

Preheat the oven to 180°C. Grease a 23cm square baking dish.

Pour the milk into a saucepan, reserving ½ cup. Whisk the cornflour and reserved milk together until smooth. Add to the milk in the saucepan. Bring to the boil over medium heat, stirring until the mixture thickens. Remove from the heat and stir in the cheese until melted. Season with salt and pepper to taste.

Pour a small amount of the soup over the base of the baking dish. Add a layer of ravioli then cover with a layer of soup. Pour over a layer of cheese sauce then another layer of ravioli. Repeat layering until all the ingredients are used, finishing with a layer of cheese sauce.

Mains

Bake for 30 minutes then sprinkle over some extra cheese. Bake for a further 20 minutes, or until the cheese is golden and bubbling. Rest for 10 minutes before serving.

TIP: Use your favourite type of ravioli, such as beef, or spinach and ricotta.

Pasta with Tomato Sauce

The tomato sauce in this recipe may seem very plain, but remember the old saying: sometimes less is more. The key here is the gentle simmering of the ingredients, which reduce in volume to a heavenly, thick and silky smooth sauce. If you would like to take this dish up a notch, purchase the best quality pasta you can afford. It makes a big difference, and it still works out to be a very economical meal.

PREP TIME
5 MINUTES

COOKING TIME
15 MINUTES

SERVES
4

INGREDIENTS

2 × 400g tins whole or chopped tomatoes

4 garlic cloves, crushed

1 tbsp white sugar

½ tsp salt

¼ cup (60ml) olive oil

20g butter

400g dried pasta (spaghetti, fettucine or pappardelle all work well)

finely grated parmesan and basil leaves, to serve (optional)

Place the tomatoes in a food processor or blender and blitz until smooth. Place the pureed tomatoes, garlic, sugar, salt and oil in a large saucepan and stir to combine. Bring to the boil then reduce the heat to low. Gently simmer, uncovered, for about 15 minutes or until the sauce has reduced by about one-third, stirring occasionally. Remove from the heat and stir through the butter.

In the meantime, cook the pasta according to the packet directions. Drain well. Serve the sauce over the pasta and sprinkle with parmesan and basil, if desired.

The sauce will keep in the fridge for up to 1 week and can be frozen for up to 3 months.

> **TIP:** If the sauce begins to splatter while simmering, half-cover the pot with a lid but ensure there's enough space for the steam to escape.

Mains

Roasted Gnocchi and Vegetables

Gnocchi is typically boiled in water; however, you may not know that gnocchi are also delicious roasted. Cooking them this way makes them crispy on the outside and soft and gooey on the inside. Bake with vegetables that are going to slightly caramelise and create a jammy sauce, and you've got a one-pan vegetarian meal everyone is going to love. Feel free to customise this recipe using other vegetables. Some suggestions are mushrooms, eggplant or capsicum, and you can add garlic, chilli and chopped fresh herbs like rosemary or thyme. You can also stir through baby spinach when you take it out of the oven.

PREP TIME
10 MINUTES

COOKING TIME
35–40 MINUTES

SERVES
4

INGREDIENTS

500g gnocchi

2 red onions, roughly chopped

250g cherry tomatoes

3 zucchini, sliced

3 tbsp olive oil

finely grated parmesan or crumbled feta, to taste

basil leaves, to serve (optional)

Preheat the oven to 180°C. Grease a baking tray and line with baking paper.

Place the gnocchi, onion, tomatoes and zucchini on the prepared tray and drizzle over the oil. Season with salt and pepper. Give everything a good mix then spread evenly on the tray.

Bake for 35–40 minutes or until the gnocchi and vegetables are cooked and starting to brown.

Serve sprinkled with parmesan or feta, and basil leaves if using.

TIP: You can buy 'shelf-fresh' gnocchi in the pasta aisle at the supermarket, or check the refrigerated section as you can find it there too.

Hawaiian Stuffed Sweet Potatoes

PREP TIME
10 MINUTES

COOKING TIME
30–40 MINUTES

SERVES
4

INGREDIENTS

2 large (250g each) sweet potatoes, scrubbed but left unpeeled

½ cup (120g) sour cream, plus extra to serve

227g tin crushed pineapple, drained

1 red onion, finely chopped

½ cup (60g) grated tasty cheese, plus extra for topping

chopped parsley, to serve (optional)

Here is an easy vegetarian recipe that will fill you up and leave you feeling very satisfied. It's an easy lunch idea or a light dinner option when paired with a salad. They are also fabulous cooked in an air fryer. Feel free to add chopped ham or cooked bacon if desired.

Preheat the oven to 180°C. Line a baking tray with baking paper.

Prick the sweet potatoes all over with a fork. Microwave for about 10 minutes, until soft and cooked through. Set aside until cool enough to handle.

Cut each sweet potato in half horizontally. Carefully scoop out the flesh, leaving a thin layer of flesh behind to keep the skin intact. Place the flesh, sour cream, pineapple, onion and cheese in a bowl and mash until well combined and creamy. Season with salt and plenty of pepper.

Place the sweet potato cases onto the prepared tray. Spoon the mixture into the cases and top with extra cheese.

Bake for 20–30 minutes or until the cheese is golden and bubbly. Leave to cool for 10 minutes. Serve warm, topped with extra sour cream, and parsley if using.

Cheese-filled Hamburger Patties

You'll be surprised at how flavoursome these patties are. The trick is to try and get the patties as thin as possible to maximise heat contact. This in turn will create a crust that is fuller in flavour compared to other patties. Serve with your favourite salad and trimmings, either in hamburger buns or just on a plate. They are also perfect to cook on the BBQ.

PREP TIME
10 MINUTES

COOKING TIME
8 MINUTES

SERVES
4

INGREDIENTS

800g beef mince

2 tsp Dijon mustard

1 cup (120g) grated cheese

vegetable oil, for frying

hamburger buns and trimmings (lettuce, red onion, tomato), to serve

Divide the mince into 8 even portions. Flatten each portion into a large, thin circle. Spread 4 of the portions with the mustard and then top with the grated cheese, leaving a 1cm border around each edge.

Top each patty with an unfilled patty, pressing the edges together until well-sealed. Season with salt and pepper on both sides.

Coat the bottom of a large frying pan with oil and place over medium-high heat. Add the patties to the pan. Cook for about 4 minutes each side or until brown and cooked through, occasionally pressing down on the patties with a metal spatula. This will help create a more flavoursome crust.

Serve on buns with all your favourite burger trimmings.

Salmon Slice

PREP TIME
10 MINUTES

COOKING TIME
45 MINUTES

SERVES
4

I always keep a tin of salmon in my pantry for this recipe. It's one of my favourite go-to meals when my pantry and fridge stocks are low. I sometimes add fresh parsley or dill, lemon pepper or lemon rind and juice, but it's also delicious as is. Serve straight from the oven, or cool and place in the fridge to eat it cold.

INGREDIENTS

1 cup (250ml) milk

1 cup (100g) dry breadcrumbs

415g tin red or pink salmon

1 cup (120g) grated tasty cheese

2 eggs, lightly beaten

Preheat the oven to 180°C. Grease a 20cm square baking dish.

Heat the milk in a saucepan until bubbles start to form. Remove from the heat, add the breadcrumbs and stir until well combined. Add the salmon, including the liquid, and mix until well combined.

Add the cheese and eggs and season with salt and pepper to taste. Mix until well combined. Pour into the prepared dish.

Bake for 45 minutes or until set and golden brown. Serve piping hot, or cold.

BBQ Satay Kebabs

PREP TIME
10 MINUTES (+30 MINUTES–8 HOURS MARINATING)

COOKING TIME
12–14 MINUTES

SERVES
4–5

Kebabs are a great, cost-effective alternative to steak as they use less meat. If you are using beef, use cuts like rump, porterhouse, sirloin or fillet. These kebabs can also be grilled in the oven, but make sure the skewers don't burn (see Tip).

INGREDIENTS

2 tbsp peanut butter (crunchy or smooth)

2 tbsp soy sauce

2 tbsp sweet chilli sauce

2 tbsp vegetable oil

700g meat of your choice, cut into 2cm cubes

coriander leaves, to serve (optional)

Place the peanut butter, soy sauce, sweet chilli sauce and oil in a large bowl and whisk until well combined. Add the meat and stir until well coated in the marinade. Cover and leave to marinate for at least 30 minutes, or place in the fridge for longer to allow the flavours to develop further (8 hours or overnight is even better).

Remove from the fridge 30 minutes before cooking to allow the meat to come to room temperature.

Preheat the BBQ to medium-high and grease the grill plate.

Thread the meat onto 8–10 bamboo or metal skewers then season with salt and pepper to taste. Cook for 12–14 minutes, turning occasionally, until the meat is cooked through and brown on all sides.

Allow to rest for 10 minutes before serving. Sprinkle with coriander leaves, if using.

TIP: If using bamboo skewers soak them in water for 20 minutes to prevent them from burning when cooking.

Sausage and Potato Bake

PREP TIME
10 MINUTES

COOKING TIME
1 HOUR 20 MINUTES

SERVES
4

Easy, economical, filling and comforting is what this recipe is all about. Of course, it can be easily adapted to suit what you have on hand. The potatoes can be replaced with any root vegetables including sweet potato, pumpkin and parsnips or a mix of whatever vegetables you have available. The stock will be absorbed into the vegetables while cooking to add amazing flavour. I like to serve this with a side of steamed greens.

INGREDIENTS

800g potatoes

1 large onion

vegetable or olive oil, for drizzling

2 tsp beef or chicken stock powder

4 tsp minced garlic

1 cup (250ml) boiling water

4–6 good quality sausages

finely chopped parsley, to serve (optional)

Preheat the oven to 180°C. Grease a roasting dish which is just big enough to fit the potatoes in a single layer.

Peel and cut the potatoes and onion into chunks and place in the roasting dish. Drizzle with a little oil, season with salt and pepper then give a good stir to coat. Bake for 20 minutes.

Meanwhile, place the stock powder and garlic in a jug. Add the boiling water and stir to combine. Cut each sausage into thirds. Scatter the sausages over the potatoes and onion, pour over the stock and give everything a good stir.

Bake uncovered for 1 hour, stirring and turning every 20 minutes, until the stock is absorbed and the potatoes and sausages are golden brown. Sprinkle with parsley to serve, if using.

Family Mince Pie

PREP TIME
15 MINUTES
(+ COOLING)

COOKING TIME
40–50 MINUTES

SERVES
4

Who can resist a good old-fashioned mince pie? This recipe can be easily adapted. You can use chicken mince and replace the roast meat gravy with roast chicken gravy. You can also add some mixed frozen vegetables before you add the soup. Try swapping the top layer of pastry with mashed potato and grated cheese, or add a layer of grated cheese under the top layer of pastry. Whatever you choose, it'll be delicious!

INGREDIENTS

2 tbsp vegetable oil

700g beef mince

1 large onion, finely chopped

24g pkt roast meat gravy mix

420g tin condensed cream of mushroom soup

2–3 sheets frozen puff pastry, just thawed

lightly beaten egg or milk for brushing pastry (optional)

Preheat the oven to 200°C. Grease a 25cm pie dish.

Heat the oil in a large pot over high heat. Add the mince and onion and cook, stirring to break up the mince, until browned. Add the gravy mix and cook for another 1 minute. Stir in the soup until everything is well combined. Remove from the heat and season with salt and pepper to taste. Allow to cool.

Line the pie dish with pastry, overlapping and trimming as needed to fit, keeping enough pastry for the top. Pour the mixture into the pastry case (see Tip). Cover the top of the pie with remaining pastry and seal the edges. Brush pastry with a little beaten egg or milk if desired, and cut small incisions in the top to allow the steam to escape.

Bake for 40–50 minutes or until the pastry is golden. Allow to cool for 10 minutes before serving.

TIP: If you cool the mixture before filling the pie, the pastry will cook and brown easier and you will avoid the pastry becoming soggy. You can also make the filling the day before and store in the fridge. This allows the flavours to develop.

SALADS

&
SIDES

Prawn and Grapefruit Cocktail

PREP TIME
15 MINUTES

COOKING TIME
0 MINUTES

SERVES
4

During the 1970s and 1980s the menu at a posh restaurant wasn't complete unless it had a prawn cocktail on it. Even if it's not fashionable these days, I still love this as an appetiser. There are many versions of this, but this one has the addition of grapefruit. It gives the cocktail a burst of tart freshness, which in turn lightens the dish and helps cut through the rich cocktail sauce. Prawn cocktails are typically served in glasses, on a bed of finely shredded iceberg lettuce. You can also sprinkle over a pinch of paprika and add a sprig of parsley as a garnish.

INGREDIENTS

500g cooked prawns, peeled, deveined and tails removed

1 grapefruit

3 tbsp mayonnaise

2 tbsp tomato sauce

1 tbsp lemon juice

shredded iceberg lettuce, paprika and finely chopped parsley, to serve (optional)

Place the prawns into a large bowl. Peel the grapefruit and cut into 1cm cubes, removing any pips. Add to the prawns and toss to combine.

Mix the mayonnaise, tomato sauce and lemon juice in a small bowl then pour over the prawns and grapefruit. Gently fold through until just combined. Season with salt and pepper.

Spoon into glasses on top of a little bed of lettuce and place in the fridge until ready to serve. Sprinkle with paprika and parsley just before serving, if using.

These are best served on the day they are made.

Corn and Tomato Summer Salad

PREP TIME
10 MINUTES

COOKING TIME
0 MINUTES

SERVES
4

Here is a light, refreshing and colourful salad option to enjoy at your next BBQ or to include as a healthy side with any meal. In this recipe I use frozen corn but feel free to use tinned or fresh corn. You can also add a handful of chopped fresh herbs like parsley, mint, basil or coriander if desired for extra flavour.

INGREDIENTS

3 cups (480g) frozen corn kernels

2 cups (320g) cherry tomatoes, quartered

1 avocado, diced

1 red onion, finely sliced

2 tbsp lime or lemon juice

1 tbsp extra virgin olive oil

Place the corn in a bowl and cover with boiling water for 5 minutes. Drain and cool.

Place all the ingredients into a salad bowl and gently toss to combine. Season with salt and pepper to taste.

Serve chilled or at room temperature.

Couscous, Pea and Feta Salad

PREP TIME
10 MINUTES

COOKING TIME
10 MINUTES

SERVES
4

I just love the freshness of this couscous salad. It has a real summer vibe to it so it's a perfect side dish at your next BBQ. It is also delicious served alongside roast lamb. It can be prepared well in advance so is perfect for entertaining. I really like the texture of Israeli couscous in this recipe; however, any couscous will work.

INGREDIENTS

1 cup (165g) Israeli (pearl) couscous

2 cups (240g) frozen peas

½ cup roughly chopped mint leaves

2 tsp finely grated lemon rind

2 tbsp lemon juice

80g feta, crumbled

1 tbsp olive oil

Cook the couscous in a large saucepan of boiling water according to the packet instructions, until tender. Drain and rinse under cold water to cool.

Cover peas in boiling water for 5 minutes to thaw, then drain and rinse under cold water to cool.

Place couscous and peas into a large bowl. Add the remaining ingredients, season with salt and pepper to taste and toss well. Refrigerate until ready to serve.

Salads & Sides

Risoni Salad

Risoni, also known as orzo, looks like large grains of rice but is actually a type of pasta. It's readily available in supermarkets and very economical. I often add some chopped cooked chicken to this salad and take a container of it into work for lunch. It keeps me satisfied all afternoon.

INGREDIENTS

½ cup (110g) risoni

1 cup (160g) cherry tomatoes, halved

1 cup roughly chopped baby spinach leaves

60g feta (or to taste), crumbled

¼ cup (60ml) balsamic vinaigrette dressing (or to taste)

Cook the risoni in a saucepan of boiling water according to the package instructions, until al dente. Drain into a sieve and rinse under cold running water to cool. Drain well.

In a large bowl, combine the cooled risoni, cherry tomatoes, baby spinach leaves and crumbled feta. Drizzle the balsamic vinaigrette dressing over and gently toss to coat evenly. Season with salt and pepper to taste.

Serve immediately or refrigerate until ready to serve.

Spinach Salad

PREP TIME
10 MINUTES

COOKING TIME
0 MINUTES

SERVES
4

The great thing about spinach is it's freely available any time of the year so it's my go-to when I'm wanting to eat salad in winter, and any other time of the year for that matter. This salad is so simple to prepare and yet punches a lot of flavour. I like to chop the spinach finely as it makes the salad denser and more flavoursome.

INGREDIENTS

120g bag baby spinach

⅓ cup (25g) finely grated parmesan

2 tbsp toasted pine nuts or chopped walnuts

2 tbsp extra virgin olive oil

1 tbsp lemon juice

Chop the spinach finely and place into a bowl. Add the parmesan and nuts and toss to combine.

Add the oil and lemon juice and toss again. Season with freshly ground pepper. Serve immediately.

> **TIP:** To toast the pine nuts or walnuts, place in a small frying pan over medium-low heat. Cook for 3–4 minutes, tossing and stirring, until golden brown. Keep a very close eye on them as they can easily burn. Transfer to a plate to cool before adding them to the salad. You can also use untoasted nuts in this recipe if preferred.

Edamame Bean and Cashew Slaw

PREP TIME
10 MINUTES

COOKING TIME
0 MINUTES

SERVES
4

I'm not one for unusual ingredients — except for this recipe. I have included this as it's just one of those recipes I can't help making repeatedly. Kewpie roasted sesame dressing can be easily sourced from most supermarkets these days and, even though it is a little more expensive than other dressings, a little does go a long way. I love every aspect of this slaw. It's fresh, salty, crunchy and can be thrown together in a matter of minutes. Feel free to play around with the ingredients.

INGREDIENTS

1 cup (120g) frozen shelled edamame beans

3 cups (240g) finely shredded green cabbage (see Tip)

½ cup (75g) roughly chopped roasted salted cashews

1 bunch coriander (stems and leaves), roughly chopped

¼ cup (60ml) Kewpie roasted sesame dressing (or to taste)

Place the edamame beans in a bowl and cover with boiling water. Stand for 5 minutes, then drain and rinse under cold water to cool.

Place the cabbage, edamame beans, cashews and coriander in a large bowl and toss to combine. Drizzle over the dressing and toss to coat. Season with salt and pepper to taste.

Serve chilled or at room temperature.

> **TIP:** If you can't be bothered with shredding cabbage then just purchase your favourite bag of ready-made coleslaw.

Chicken and Cashew Salad

PREP TIME
15 MINUTES

COOKING TIME
0 MINUTES

SERVES
2–3

This salad is a great way to use up any leftover roast or rotisserie chicken. In saying that, I have been known to purchase a rotisserie chicken especially for this salad. I love the freshness the apple and celery play in this dish and then the cashews add a salty crunch. I like to dice the ingredients into quite small, similar-sized chunks so you can get all the ingredients in one mouthful. Take it chilled to your next picnic or serve on a bed of salad greens, alongside some fresh buns for an alfresco lunch or a light summer dinner.

INGREDIENTS

2 cups (320g) finely diced cooked chicken

1 red apple, finely diced

1 cup (140g) finely diced celery

1 cup (150g) chopped roasted, salted cashews

¼–½ cup (75g–150g) mayonnaise (to your liking)

Place all the ingredients into a large bowl and mix to combine. Season with salt and pepper to taste.

Transfer to a serving bowl or plate. Cover and chill in the fridge until ready to serve. This is best eaten on the day it is made.

VARIATIONS:
- Swap apple for grapes.
- Swap cashews for toasted walnuts.
- Swap mayonnaise for plain Greek yoghurt and a squeeze of lemon juice for a lighter version, or use half mayonnaise and half yoghurt.

Balsamic-roasted Tomatoes and Zucchini

PREP TIME
10 MINUTES

COOKING TIME
25–30 MINUTES

SERVES
4

Here is an easy way to use up your tomatoes and zucchini in summer when they are most plentiful. I sometimes add a chopped red onion to the mix for extra flavour; however, this is not necessary. Serve warm as a side dish or toss through cooked pasta for an easy vegetarian dinner. You can also cool them and toss through salad greens.

INGREDIENTS

4 zucchini, thickly sliced

2 cups (320g) cherry tomatoes

2 tbsp olive oil

1 tbsp runny honey

1 tbsp balsamic vinegar

½ tsp each salt and pepper

chopped parsley, to serve (optional)

Preheat oven to 200°C. Grease a baking tray and line with baking paper.

Place all the ingredients in a large bowl and toss to ensure the vegetables are well coated in the oil, honey and vinegar. Tip the vegetables onto the prepared tray and distribute evenly.

Bake for 25–30 minutes, turning halfway through cooking, until the vegetables are cooked through and starting to caramelise.

Serve warm or at room temperature, sprinkled with parsley if using.

Baked Rice

PREP TIME
5 MINUTES

COOKING TIME
20–25 MINUTES

SERVES
4

If you've never baked rice before then give this a go. I always cook rice this way when I have my oven on cooking a casserole or any other dish that requires rice. In fact, I will turn my oven on specially to make it this way. The result is light, fluffy rice with a slight nutty flavour to it. It's simply delicious and I'm sure it will become a favourite of yours too! You can also cook brown rice this way but just add an extra 10 minutes or so to the cooking time.

INGREDIENTS

1 cup (200g) basmati rice, washed and drained

2 cups (500ml) boiling water

1 tbsp butter

½ tsp salt

Preheat the oven to 180°C.

Place all the ingredients into an ovenproof dish and give a quick stir to combine. Cover with a lid or foil.

Bake for 20–25 minutes or until light and fluffy. Take care when uncovering as steam will escape.

Curried Potato Wedges

PREP TIME
10 MINUTES

COOKING TIME
40–45 MINUTES

SERVES
4

Wedges are a very popular side dish suitable for almost any occasion. They also make a satisfying snack with drinks — especially when sitting in front of the TV watching your favourite footy game!

INGREDIENTS

4 large potatoes

2 tbsp vegetable oil

2 tsp paprika

1 tsp curry powder

½–1 tsp salt (to taste)

aioli, sour cream or yoghurt, to serve (optional)

Preheat the oven to 200°C. Grease a large baking tray.

Scrub the potatoes (but do not peel) and cut into wedges. Place into a large bowl. Drizzle the oil over and toss until the potatoes are well coated.

Mix the paprika, curry powder and salt together in a small bowl then sprinkle over the potatoes. Mix until the potatoes are evenly coated.

Spread the potatoes in a single layer on the baking tray, making sure they do not touch each other.

Bake for 40–45 minutes, turning halfway through cooking. Set aside for 5 minutes to cool slightly, then serve with aioli, sour cream or yoghurt.

Flash Potato Mash

PREP TIME
10 MINUTES

COOKING TIME
15 MINUTES

SERVES
4

The addition of these extra ingredients will take your humble mashed potatoes to a level good enough to serve at a dinner party. You can also use sweet potato, parsnips or pumpkin as an alternative to potatoes. My daughter-in-law loves this and often requests it when she comes for dinner.
Of course, there are never any complaints!

INGREDIENTS

800g starchy potatoes (such as Agria), peeled and cut into chunks

½ red onion, finely chopped

100g feta, crumbled

½ cup finely chopped parsley

Place the potatoes into a large pot of salted water and bring to the boil. Cook for 10–15 minutes or until tender. Drain well and mash to your liking.

Stir through the onion, feta and parsley. Season with salt and pepper to taste and serve immediately.

Leftovers can be stored, covered, in the fridge for up to 2 days and reheated in the microwave when ready to consume.

Quick Potato Bake

PREP TIME
15 MINUTES

COOKING TIME
45 MINUTES

SERVES
4

A potato bake is a must in your recipe repertoire. This one is quicker to make than a normal potato bake, with the help of your microwave. It's also a lot easier than a potato gratin as you don't need to slice the potatoes thinly and then layer them. Just chop into cubes and throw into your baking dish. Couldn't be easier!

INGREDIENTS

800g roasting potatoes, peeled and chopped into 1cm cubes

30g butter, melted

30g pkt dried French onion soup mix

1 cup (250ml) cream or milk, or a mixture of both

1 cup (120g) grated tasty cheese

Preheat the oven to 180°C. Grease a 20cm square microwave-safe baking dish.

Place the potatoes into the prepared dish. Pour over the butter and season with salt and pepper to taste. Mix to combine, then microwave uncovered on high for 15 minutes.

In the meantime, add the soup mix to the milk or cream and mix until well combined. Pour over the potatoes then sprinkle the cheese over the top.

Bake for 30 minutes or until the cheese is golden and the mixture is bubbling. Stand for 5 minutes before serving.

No-knead Cheese and Onion Bread

PREP TIME
5 MINUTES
(+ 70 MINUTES
ACTIVATING
AND RISING)

COOKING TIME
25 MINUTES

SERVES
8

INGREDIENTS

2 tsp dry yeast

1 tsp white sugar

3 cups (450g) plain flour

30g pkt dried French onion soup mix

1 cup (120g) grated tasty cheese

There is something very satisfying about making your own bread, and this recipe couldn't be easier. You'll not only impress yourself but also your family and friends, and your kitchen is going to smell like a bakery. Enjoy it fresh and warm, or toasted with a spread of butter. Add your favourite savoury toppings or serve alongside a bowl of soup. Feel free to add cooked chopped onion or bacon or even extras like ham and chopped fresh herbs.

Grease a loaf pan and line with baking paper.

Pour 1½ cups (375ml) lukewarm water into a large bowl. Add the yeast and sugar and stir to dissolve. Leave to activate for about 10 minutes (small bubbles should form).

Add the remaining ingredients and stir until a dough forms. Tip into the prepared pan, cover with a tea towel and leave in a warm, draught-free place for about 1 hour or until doubled in size.

Meanwhile, preheat the oven to 200°C.

Bake the loaf for 25 minutes or until the top makes a hollow sound when tapped.

Eat fresh from the oven or keep in the fridge for 2–3 days. It can also be frozen for up to 2 months.

Easy Focaccia

PREP TIME
5 MINUTES
(+ 90 MINUTES
ACTIVATING
AND RISING)

COOKING TIME
15–20 MINUTES

SERVES
6

If you have never tried your hand at breadmaking before then this is a great recipe to start with. With only 5 minutes' hands-on time, and using this simple technique, you'll be wondering why it's taken you so long to give it a go. Cut this into little chunks for a delicious appetiser with drinks, serve slices alongside your favourite soup (or any meal), or just eat it anytime because it's totally delicious! Feel free to add extras on top before baking, like chopped fresh rosemary, olives, garlic, sundried tomatoes, cherry tomatoes, caramelised onions — the sky's the limit.

INGREDIENTS

1 tsp dry yeast

1 tsp white sugar

2½ cups (375g) plain flour

1 tsp salt

4 tbsp extra virgin olive oil, plus extra for greasing

flaky or coarse sea salt

fresh rosemary (optional)

Pour 1½ cups (375ml) lukewarm water into a large bowl. Add the yeast and sugar and stir to dissolve. Leave to activate for about 10 minutes (small bubbles should form).

Add the flour and salt and stir until a dough forms – the mixture will be very wet. Place 2 tbsp of the oil into another large bowl. Tip the dough into the bowl and turn to coat in the oil. Cover with a tea towel and leave in a warm draught-free place for about 1 hour or until doubled in size.

Meanwhile, preheat oven to 220°C. Grease a 20cm × 30cm baking dish and line with baking paper, then grease the paper well with olive oil.

Now here's the secret step to ensuring the perfect focaccia. Once the dough has risen, take an edge and fold it into the centre. Give the bowl a quarter turn and do another fold. Repeat twice more, so you have four sides folded into the middle.

Tip the mixture into the prepared dish (smooth side up) and spread out to cover the base. Cover and let rest in a warm place for another 20 minutes.

Using oiled fingertips, press holes all over the dough. Drizzle with the remaining olive oil and sprinkle with sea salt, and rosemary if using. Bake for 15–20 minutes or until golden brown.

Serve warm or at room temperature. It's best eaten the day it's made but can be frozen for up to 1 month.

Olive Oil and Balsamic Dipping Sauce

PREP TIME
10 MINUTES
(+ COOLING)

COOKING TIME
2 MINUTES

SERVES
4

For me, one of the joys of eating at an Italian restaurant is ordering bread with dipping sauce. Luckily, you don't need to be at a fancy restaurant to enjoy this popular appetiser. It's so easy to make and perfect to serve with drinks at your next dinner party. Feel free to add fresh chopped chilli or chilli flakes if you would like some heat. Serve with warm slices of ciabatta or focaccia (recipe page 158) and watch it disappear.

INGREDIENTS

½ cup (125ml) extra virgin olive oil

3 garlic cloves, crushed

3 tbsp balsamic vinegar

½ tsp dried thyme, basil, rosemary or oregano

¼ cup (20g) finely grated parmesan cheese (optional)

Heat the oil in a small frying pan or saucepan over medium heat until hot but not boiling. Remove from the heat, add the garlic and stir for about 1 minute, until the garlic is fragrant. Pour into a serving bowl and allow to cool.

Add the remaining ingredients and mix to combine. Season with salt and pepper to taste. Serve with warm bread for dipping.

Store leftovers in an airtight container in the fridge for up to 3 days and bring to room temperature before serving. The oil may harden in the fridge but will liquify once back at room temperature.

DES

SERTS

Baked Custard

PREP TIME
10 MINUTES

COOKING TIME
35–40 MINUTES

SERVES
4

This old-fashioned recipe has been around for generations, and it screams comfort. It's smooth, creamy and so easy to prepare. What I love about this dessert is it's not laden with loads of sugar but has just enough to satisfy your sweet tooth. Serve on its own, or with fresh berries or preserved fruit.

INGREDIENTS

2 cups (500ml) milk or cream, or a combination of both

⅓ cup (75g) caster sugar

3 eggs, plus 1 egg yolk

1 tsp vanilla extract

freshly grated nutmeg, to taste

Preheat the oven to 160°C.

Combine the milk or cream and the sugar in a saucepan. Stir over medium heat until the sugar has dissolved and the mixture is just below boiling point. Remove from the heat.

Whisk the eggs, yolk and vanilla in a large bowl until just combined (do not allow the eggs to become frothy). Gradually add the hot milk, stirring constantly, until combined. Pour the mixture through a sieve into a 4-cup capacity baking dish. Lightly dust the top with nutmeg.

Place the dish into a roasting pan and carefully fill the pan with boiling water until it comes halfway up the sides of the dish. Bake for 35–40 minutes, until the custard is set but still a little wobbly in the centre.

Serve warm, or allow to cool and then place in the fridge to serve chilled.

Keep in the fridge for up to 2 days.

Desserts

Chocolate Mousse

PREP TIME
10 MINUTES

SETTING TIME
2 HOURS

SERVES
4–5

This chocolate mousse is a little denser than most recipes as it does not contain beaten egg whites. It results in a much richer consistency and stronger chocolate flavour, but it's just as smooth and silky as traditional recipes. You also serve this in a smaller quantity than you would normal chocolate mousse due to its richness. It makes the perfect dinner party dessert as it can be made well ahead of time. Adding 1 tsp vanilla extract will add extra flavour if desired.

INGREDIENTS

170g dark chocolate

1 tbsp icing sugar

25g butter

2 egg yolks, at room temperature

1 cup (250ml) cream

¼ tsp salt

whipped cream, mint leaves and grated chocolate, to serve (optional)

Break the chocolate into small pieces. Place into a large microwave-safe bowl with the icing sugar and butter. Heat in the microwave, using 30-second bursts, until just melted. Stir to combine. Cool slightly.

Beat in the egg yolks one at a time until well combined. Whip the cream in a separate bowl then add to the chocolate mixture along with the salt. Fold together until just combined.

Spoon into small glasses or bowls. Place in the fridge for about 2 hours, until set. Serve topped with whipped cream, mint leaves and grated chocolate, if using.

Keep in the fridge for up to 3 days.

TIP: I like to serve these in liqueur glasses, which you can pick up cheaply from second-hand stores. Then I put any extra mousse in a bowl for people to help themselves to seconds.

Boysenberry Delight

PREP TIME
5 MINUTES

COOKING TIME
5 MINUTES (+ 2
HOURS SETTING)

SERVES
4

This cheerful dessert is made in a flash and uses only 3 ingredients. It's the perfect dessert to serve any time of the year and is popular with both adults and children. It can be set either in one bowl or in individual glasses.

INGREDIENTS

425g tin boysenberries

85g pkt blackberry jelly crystals

500ml vanilla ice cream

whipped cream, to serve

Place the boysenberries, including the juice, and jelly crystals in a large saucepan, reserving some berries to serve. Slowly bring to the boil, stirring until the jelly has dissolved. Remove from the heat and stir in the ice cream. Keep stirring until the ice cream has melted and is fully incorporated into the berry mixture.

Pour into a serving bowl or individual serving glasses. Place in the fridge for at least 2 hours, to set.

Serve topped with whipped cream and reserved boysenberries.

Keep in the fridge for up to 1 day.

Creamy Chocolate Ripple Dessert

PREP TIME
15 MINUTES

SETTING TIME
3 HOURS

SERVES
4–6

I have made this old-fashioned chocolate ripple dessert even easier by constructing it in a dish as opposed to forming it into a log. If you would like to make it child-friendly then dip the biscuits in orange juice, Milo or milk. For a decadent, adults-only dessert, replace the coffee with Irish cream.

INGREDIENTS

300ml cream

2 tbsp icing sugar

300g chocolate chip cookies

½ cup (125ml) strong coffee, cooled

grated chocolate, for sprinkling

Place the cream and icing sugar in a bowl and use electric beaters to beat until firm peaks form.

Working one at a time, briefly dip ⅓ of the cookies into the coffee on both sides. Arrange in a single layer over the base of a 20cm square serving dish. Spread over ⅓ of the cream.

Repeat the layers another two times, finishing with a layer of cream. Sprinkle over the grated chocolate. Place in the fridge for at least 3 hours, to allow the biscuits to soften and the dessert to set.

Cut into squares to serve.

Keep in the fridge for up to 1 day.

Creamy Lemon Pudding

I was given this recipe over 35 years ago from an old work colleague. It's one of those recipes I have used many times when I have had little time or limited enthusiasm to make a dessert. It's creamy, sweet and tart and always goes down a treat. It's also a very easy recipe to adapt to any number of servings so perfect for entertaining a crowd, large or small. I like to serve this in glasses topped with a dollop of extra cream and a few berries.

PREP TIME
10 MINUTES

SETTING TIME
2 HOURS

SERVES
6

INGREDIENTS

2 cups (500ml) cream

200g (½ 395g tin) sweetened condensed milk

1 tsp finely grated lemon rind

½ cup (125ml) lemon juice

whipped cream, berries and shredded lemon rind, to serve (optional)

Place cream, sweetened condensed milk, grated lemon rind and juice into a bowl and, using an electric or hand-held beater, beat until soft peaks form. Spoon into serving glasses.

Place into the fridge for about 2 hours, until set.

To serve, top with whipped cream, berries and shredded lemon rind, if using.

Keep in the fridge for up to 1 day.

Healthy Whipped Cottage Cheese Pudding

PREP TIME
5 MINUTES

SETTING TIME
1 HOUR

SERVES
2–3

If you're after a dessert without the guilt then look no further than this recipe. It's protein-rich and refined sugar-free but very satisfying with its sweet, creamy consistency. If someone is not a fan of cottage cheese, don't worry. They won't even know it's the main ingredient. If you like you could serve this with a dusting of cocoa powder and/or topped with berries. Adding cocoa or cacao will add a deliciously dark tint to the pudding (as pictured).

INGREDIENTS

250g cottage cheese

2 tbsp pure maple syrup

1 banana

2 tbsp cocoa or cacao powder (optional)

1 tsp vanilla extract

unsweetened yoghurt and grated dark chocolate, to serve (optional)

Place all the ingredients in a blender or food processor and blitz for a minute or two until a thick, creamy consistency is achieved.

Spoon into serving glasses or dishes and place in the fridge for at least an hour to firm up.

Serve topped with yoghurt and grated dark chocolate, if using.

These will keep in the fridge for up to 3 days.

Poires Belle Hélène
(Pears with Chocolate Sauce)

PREP TIME
10 MINUTES

COOKING TIME
5 MINUTES

SERVES
4

If you want to sound like a master chef, tell your guests you're going to whip them up a Poires Belle Hélène dessert. It's the French way of saying 'pears with chocolate sauce' and it couldn't be quicker or easier with this creative version. Traditionally the recipe requires the pears to be poached in a spice-infused syrup, but using tinned pears cuts down the work and is still decadent and delicious.

INGREDIENTS

825g tin pear slices in juice

120g dark chocolate, broken into small pieces

35g butter

pinch of salt

vanilla ice cream, to serve (optional)

Drain the pears, reserving 5 tbsp of the juice. Divide the pears among 4 dessert plates.

Place the reserved juice, chocolate, butter and salt into a small saucepan. Stir constantly over low heat until the chocolate and butter have melted and the mixture is evenly combined.

Remove from the heat and pour over the pears. Serve immediately, with ice cream if using.

Salted Caramel Ice Cream

PREP TIME
5 MINUTES

FREEZING TIME
4 HOURS

SERVES
6

If you can find an easier recipe for ice cream than this one, I'll eat my hat! Simply beat the caramel and cream, add salt, and freeze. No ice cream maker needed and it's simply delicious. A fun serving option is to sandwich a scoop of ice cream between 2 of your favourite cookies.

INGREDIENTS

2 cups (500ml) cream

200g (½ 395g tin) caramel filling (see Tip)

½–¾ tsp sea salt or Himalayan salt

chocolate sauce and extra sea salt or Himalayan salt, to serve (optional)

Place the cream and caramel in a bowl. Use electric beaters to beat until soft peaks form (it should be the consistency of whipped cream). Gently fold in the salt. Spoon into a freezer-safe container.

Freeze for 4 hours or until solid. Take it out of the freezer 10 minutes before serving to soften slightly.

Scoop into serving dishes. Drizzle with chocolate sauce and sprinkle with a little extra salt, if using.

You can keep this in the freezer for up to 3 months, but I doubt it'll be around for that long!

> **TIP:** Use the other half of the tin of caramel filling to make my caramel cookies on page 26.

Desserts

Lemon Meringue Ice Cream Loaf

PREP TIME
10 MINUTES

FREEZING TIME
6 HOURS

SERVES
8

The use of store-bought meringues and lemon curd makes this dessert convenient and super easy to make. It is creamy, not overly sweet, with a refreshing tang and a little crunch to it. A perfect summer dessert.

INGREDIENTS

1 cup (250ml) cream

1 cup (280g) plain unsweetened yoghurt

1 tbsp finely grated lemon rind

4 tbsp lemon curd, plus extra to serve

90g meringue nests, lightly crushed, plus extra to serve (see Tip)

shredded lemon rind, to serve (optional)

Line a loaf pan with plastic wrap.

Place the cream and yoghurt in a bowl and beat until soft peaks form. Fold in the grated lemon rind, lemon curd and crushed meringues. Spoon the mixture into the prepared pan and spread out evenly. Cover with another layer of plastic wrap.

Freeze for at least 6 hours or until firm. When ready to serve, take the plastic wrap off the top and lay a serving dish over the loaf pan. Carefully flip to unmould the loaf. Remove the rest of the plastic wrap.

Top with extra lemon curd, sprinkle with extra crushed meringues and shredded lemon rind. Cut into slices and serve immediately.

This dessert will keep in the freezer for up to 6 weeks.

> **TIP:** Don't crush the meringue too finely. You still want some bigger pieces.

Apple Strudel

PREP TIME
10 MINUTES

COOKING TIME
30–35 MINUTES

SERVES
3–4

INGREDIENTS

1 sheet frozen puff pastry, just thawed

3 cooking apples (I like to use Granny Smiths)

¼ cup (55g) brown sugar

1 tsp cornflour

½ tsp ground cinnamon

1 tbsp raisins (optional)

milk to brush (optional)

If you find making apple pie too fiddly then give apple strudel a go instead. With a few simple ingredients you can create this comforting dessert that always goes down a treat. I love to serve this dessert warm, with a scoop of vanilla ice cream on the side.

Preheat the oven to 200°C. Grease a baking tray and line with baking paper.

Place the pastry onto the prepared tray. Peel and grate the apples, then use your hands to squeeze the excess juice into a glass (it's delicious to drink, so don't waste it).

Place the apples into a bowl then add the sugar, cornflour, cinnamon and raisins, if using. Mix to combine.

Spoon the apple mixture evenly over one half of the pastry, leaving a 1cm border on 3 sides. Fold the other half of the pastry over the apples and press or crimp the edges to seal. Brush the top with a little milk if desired. Prick the top of the pastry with a fork 4–5 times to allow the steam to escape.

Bake for 30–35 minutes, until the pastry is golden. Remove from the oven and allow to cool for at least 15 minutes before serving.

Banoffee Pie

If you want to serve a showstopper dessert with minimal effort at your next dinner party, then why not give this a go. With its biscuit base and gooey caramel centre, you're guaranteed to make your guests go home with smiles on their faces!

PREP TIME
10 MINUTES

FREEZING TIME
30 MINUTES

SERVES
6

INGREDIENTS

250g plain sweet biscuits, crushed

120g butter, melted and cooled

395g tin caramel filling

2–3 bananas

1 cup (250ml) cream

extra sliced banana and grated chocolate, to serve (optional)

Grease the base of a 20cm round springform cake pan.

Place the crushed biscuits and melted butter in a bowl and mix until well combined. Tip the biscuit mixture into the base of the prepared pan and press out evenly. Place in the freezer for 30 minutes.

Remove from the freezer and spoon the caramel filling evenly on top of the biscuit base. Slice the bananas and layer over the caramel. Whip the cream, then spoon evenly over the bananas. Refrigerate until ready to serve, but this should be made the day it is served.

Run a knife around the edge of the pie and remove the side of the pan. Run a knife between the biscuit base and the pan base to loosen, then carefully slide the pie onto a serving plate.

Serve topped with extra banana slices and grated chocolate, if using.

Crustless Yoghurt and Blueberry Tart

PREP TIME
10 MINUTES

COOKING TIME
30–40 MINUTES

SERVES
6

If you love a traditional clafoutis then I'm sure you'll love this yoghurt and blueberry tart. It has a similar consistency to clafoutis, like a thick, dense pancake. I love the fact it's not overly sweet and is best made a day in advance. Perfect for entertaining. As an added advantage, this recipe is gluten-free. Feel free to use other berries if you don't have blueberries. I like to serve this with extra Greek yoghurt and berries on top.

INGREDIENTS

2 cups (560g) plain unsweetened Greek yoghurt

½ cup (110g) caster sugar

⅓ cup (50g) cornflour

6 egg yolks

1 tsp vanilla extract (optional)

1 cup (150g) blueberries (thawed frozen or fresh)

extra plain unsweetened Greek yoghurt and blueberries to serve (optional)

Preheat oven to 180°C. Grease the base and sides of a 20cm round springform cake pan. Line the base with baking paper.

Place all the ingredients, except the blueberries, into a bowl and whisk until well combined. Pour into the prepared pan. Scatter the blueberries evenly over the top of the mixture (they will sink slightly).

Bake for 30–40 minutes or until golden and set. Cool in the pan then cover and place in the fridge until ready to serve.

Top with extra yoghurt and blueberries, if using, and cut into wedges to serve.

Three-ingredient Peach Cobbler

PREP TIME
5 MINUTES

COOKING TIME
40–50 MINUTES

SERVES
6–8

Old-fashioned peach cobbler is made even easier with the use of packet cake mix. The great thing about this recipe is you can get quite creative with it. I have made this recipe multiple times using different tinned fruit like plums, apricots, pears or cherries. A handful of berries thrown in is also delicious. I have also used chocolate cake mix instead of vanilla, which is equally delicious. Dust with a little icing sugar before serving if desired. Devour while warm. You could have this with runny cream or whipped cream instead of ice cream, if you prefer.

INGREDIENTS

820g (or 2 × 400g) tin peach slices in juice

540g pkt vanilla cake mix

120g butter, melted

vanilla ice cream, to serve

Preheat the oven to 180°C. Grease a 23cm square baking dish.

Tip the peaches (including the juice) into the dish and spread out evenly. Place the cake mix and butter into a bowl and mix until combined. Scatter the mixture over the peaches. It doesn't matter if the mixture doesn't completely cover the peaches.

Bake for 40–50 minutes until golden and bubbling.

Stand for 5 minutes, then serve with vanilla ice cream.

Desserts

Peach Galette

A fruit galette is a tart made with sweetened fruit encased in pastry. It's so easy to put together and it doesn't matter if it doesn't look perfect as it's supposed to be rustic. In this recipe I am using tinned peaches but you can also use fresh peaches, apricots or nectarines. Sometimes I'll also throw in a handful of berries (fresh or thawed from frozen) if I have them on hand.

PREP TIME
10 MINUTES

COOKING TIME
35–40 MINUTES

SERVES
4

INGREDIENTS

1 sheet frozen puff pastry, just thawed

820g tin peaches, drained and cut into 1cm pieces

3 tbsp brown sugar

1 tbsp cornflour

½ tsp ground cinnamon

beaten egg or milk, to glaze (optional)

vanilla ice cream or whipped cream, to serve

Preheat the oven to 180°C. Grease a baking tray and line with baking paper.

Place the puff pastry in the centre of the prepared tray and trim the corners to make a large circle.

Combine the remaining ingredients in a large bowl and toss to coat. Tip the mixture onto the pastry, leaving a 4cm border around the edge.

Fold the pastry just over the peaches, making pleats by pinching the dough together with your fingers. Brush the pastry with a little beaten egg or milk.

Bake for 35–40 minutes or until the crust is golden.

Cool for 10 minutes before serving. Serve warm or at room temperature, with a scoop of vanilla ice cream or whipped cream.

Basque Cheesecake

<u>PREP TIME</u>
10 MINUTES
(+ COOLING)

<u>COOKING TIME</u>
45–50 MINUTES
(+ 3 HOURS
CHILLING)

<u>SERVES</u>
8

INGREDIENTS

500g cream cheese, chopped, at room temperature

4 eggs, at room temperature

1 cup (220g) caster sugar

1 cup (250ml) cream

1 tsp vanilla extract

¼ tsp salt

plain yoghurt, blueberries and shredded lemon rind, to serve (optional)

Basque cheesecake is a Spanish dessert that is lighter in texture compared to the classic New York cheesecake. It's rich, gooey and slightly caramelised around the edges. It truly is heaven on a plate! I like to serve this with plain yoghurt and fresh berries to help balance out the richness. It can be made a day or two in advance, so it's perfect for entertaining. It does make a large dessert but you can freeze any leftovers for up to 3 months.

Preheat the oven to 200°C. Grease a 20cm springform pan and line with baking paper.

Use electric beaters to beat the cream cheese until smooth. Add the eggs one at a time, making sure each is well incorporated before adding the next one. Add the sugar in a slow stream to ensure it is well incorporated, then add the rest of the ingredients and beat until well combined. Pour into the prepared pan.

Bake for 45–50 minutes, until the top is golden and the edges are caramelised. The centre will still be a little wobbly.

Leave in the pan to cool completely then place in the fridge to chill at least 3 hours, until ready to serve. It is normal for the cheesecake to sink when cooling.

Serve topped with yoghurt, berries and shredded lemon rind, if using.

Desserts

Whole Orange Cake with Orange Glaze

PREP TIME
5 MINUTES

COOKING TIME
30–35 MINUTES

SERVES
10–12

Here's a cake that will be oven-ready within 5 minutes. It's a deliciously moist cake packed full of orange flavour. I know it seems unusual using a whole orange, but it works! For added flavour you can also add a teaspoon of vanilla or almond extract, but it's delicious just as it is too. Enjoy a slice with a dollop of whipped cream or yoghurt on the side.

INGREDIENTS

1 whole orange

125g butter, melted and cooled (see Tip)

2 eggs

1 cup (220g) white sugar

1 tsp vanilla or almond extract (optional)

1½ cups (225g) self-raising flour

ORANGE GLAZE

½ cup (110g) white sugar

¼ cup (60ml) orange juice

shredded rind of 1 orange

Preheat the oven to 180°C. Grease a 23cm round cake pan and line with baking paper.

Wash the orange and remove the stem. Cut into quarters, remove any pips and place into a food processor or blender. Blitz until the orange is pureed. Add the butter, eggs, sugar and extract if using, and blitz again until well blended.

Add the flour and pulse until just combined. Tip the mixture into the prepared pan, spreading it out evenly.

Bake for 30–35 minutes or until a skewer inserted into the centre comes out clean.

Just before the cake is ready, make the orange glaze. Place all the ingredients into a small saucepan and stir over medium heat until the sugar has dissolved.

Remove the cake from the oven and poke holes over the top of the cake with a skewer or toothpick. Pour the hot glaze over the cake. Allow the cake to cool completely in the pan, then turn out.

Store in an airtight container at room temperature for up to 1 week, or freeze for up to 2 months.

TIP: Replace the butter with ½ cup (125ml) neutral oil, such as canola, vegetable or grapeseed, if you like.

ACKNOWLEDGEMENTS

I would like to sincerely thank Alex Hedley from HarperCollins Publishers for asking me to write this cookbook for them. Up until now I have self-published my cookbooks so this is a new journey for me. Thank you for believing in me and encouraging me along the way. It has been an honour working with such a distinguished publishing house, alongside a team of amazing professionals.

Thank you to my photographer, Olivia Moore, owner of That Green Olive. Your ability to capture the essence of each dish through your lens brings my recipes to life. You are a delight and pleasure to work with.

I am profoundly grateful for the unwavering support, encouragement and dedication my husband Wayne has shown me throughout this journey of creating this cookbook. From cleaning up after my long days of recipe testing and photographing, to your willingness to taste countless dishes and provide honest feedback, you have significantly enriched the content of this cookbook. Your belief in me, even during moments of self-doubt, has given me the confidence to pursue my passion and turn it into a reality.

INDEX

INDEX

A

B

C

P

Parmesan and mustard lamb chops 91

Pasta

gnocchi and vegetables, roasted 110

macaroni and cheese 99

prawn and lemon risoni, baked 102

ravioli lasagne 106

risoni salad 134

with tomato sauce 109

Pea, couscous and feta salad 133

Peach

cobbler 193

galette 194

Peanut butter muesli bars 46

Peanut, satay kebabs 120

Pears with chocolate sauce 179

Pie

banoffee 187

mince (savoury) 124

peach cobbler 193

sausage (savoury) 96

see also tart

Pineapple

beef casserole 81

stuffed sweet potatoes 113

Pine nuts, spinach salad 137

Poires belle Hélène (pears with chocolate sauce) 179

Pork rissoles 95

Potato

baked 154

breakfast bake 14

mashed 151

and sausage bake 123

wedges, curried 148

Prawn

and grapefruit cocktail 129

and lemon risoni 102

Pudding

cottage cheese 174

lemon 173

Pumpkin risotto 105

R

Ravioli lasagne 106

Rice

baked 147

pumpkin risotto 105

Risoni

prawn and lemon 102

salad 134

Risotto, baked pumpkin 105

Rissoles, pork 95

Roasted gnocchi and vegetables 110

S

Salad

chicken and cashew 143

corn and tomato 130

couscous, pea and feta 133

edamame bean and cashew 138

risoni 134

spinach 137

Salmon

baked, japanese-inspired 60

slice 119

Salted caramel ice cream 180

Satay kebabs, BBQ 120

Sausage

pie 96

and potato bake 123

Scones with cream 40

Scrolls, cheese and vegemite 22

Slice

chocolate cornflake 50

HarperCollins*Publishers*
Australia • Brazil • Canada • France • Germany • Holland • India
Italy • Japan • Mexico • New Zealand • Poland • Spain • Sweden
Switzerland • United Kingdom • United States of America

First published in 2024
by HarperCollins*Publishers* (New Zealand) Limited
Unit D1, 63 Apollo Drive, Rosedale, Auckland 0632, New Zealand
harpercollins.co.nz

A catalogue record for this book is available from the National Library of New Zealand

ISBN 978 1 7755 4243 8 (paperback)
ISBN 978 1 7754 9274 0 (ebook)

Project editor: Shannon Kelly
Copy editor: Tracy Rutherford
Cover and internal design by Mietta Yans, HarperCollins Design Studio
Food photography: Olivia Moore, That Green Olive
Front cover images (clockwise from top left): Lemon, Basil and Feta Chicken (page 67);
Edamame Bean and Cashew Slaw (page 138); Tuscan Yoghurt-marinated Chicken (page 78);
Leftovers Fritters (page 17); Basque Cheesecake (page 197);
Back cover images (left to right): Bacon-wrapped Chicken (page 63); Poires Belle Hélène (page 179);
Corn and Tomato Summer Salad (page 130)
Photograph of author by Mark Duncan, Day Off Studio
Index by Shannon Kelly
Colour reproduction by Splitting Image Colour Studio, Wantirna, Victoria
Printed and bound in China

8 7 6 5 4 3 2 1   24 25 26 27 28